COLLEGE STRESS
SOLUTIONS

COLLEGE STRESS
SOLUTIONS

STRESS MANAGEMENT TECHNIQUES to
▸ Beat Anxiety ▸ Make the Grade
▸ Enjoy the Full College Experience

KELCI LYNN LUCIER, EdM

Adamsmedia
Avon, Massachusetts

Published by
Adams Media, a division of F+W Media, Inc.
57 Littlefield Street, Avon, MA 02322. U.S.A.
www.adamsmedia.com

ISBN 10: 1-4405-7082-5
ISBN 13: 978-1-4405-7082-7
eISBN 10: 1-4405-7091-4
eISBN 13: 978-1-4405-7091-9

Printed in the United States of America.

10   9   8   7   6   5   4   3   2   1

Library of Congress Cataloging-in-Publication Data
Lucier, Kelci Lynn.
    College stress solutions / Kelci Lynn Lucier.
        pages cm
    Includes index.
    ISBN-13: 978-1-4405-7082-7 (pb)
    ISBN-10: 1-4405-7082-5 (pb)
    ISBN-13: 978-1-4405-7091-9 (ebook)
    ISBN-10: 1-4405-7091-4 (ebook)
    1. College students--United States--Psychology. 2. Stress (Psychology)--Prevention. I. Title.
    LA229.L83 2014
    378.1'98--dc23

2013044590

This book is intended as general information only and should not be used to diagnose or treat any health condition. This book does not provide medical advice and is not intended to replace the advice of a medical professional. Consult your physician about any condition that may require diagnosis or medical attention.

Many of the designations used by manufacturers and sellers to distinguish their product are claimed as trademarks. Where those designations appear in this book and F+W Media, Inc. was aware of a trademark claim, the designations have been printed with initial capital letters.

Cover design by Sylvia McArdle.
Cover images © 123rf.com/Syda Productions/Ferli Achirulli.

*This book is available at quantity discounts for bulk purchases.
For information, please call 1-800-289-0963.*

CONTENTS

Dedication

To David, Samuel, & Elizabeth

Acknowledgments

It's difficult to know where to start when it comes to thanking people for helping you write your first book.

First, to Adams Media for expressing interest in the book and in having me as the author, and in particular to my editors, Brendan O'Neill and Laura Daly, for their tireless support and patience when answering my incessant questions.

The book also wouldn't be anywhere near as detailed as it is without the help of countless people I interviewed, some of whom are quoted, some of whom are not, but all of whom are appreciated. Karen Boss, Thomas L. Burkdall, John H. Carothers, Shareia N. Carter, Soyoung Amy Choi-Won, Ellen Kelly Daley, Janice DeMonsi, Jeanette Duffels, Grace Flowers, Travis Greene, Steve Hairston, Ryan-Jasen Andeis Henne, Kurt C. Holmes, Liz Josefsberg, Debbie Kaylor, Brynn Kimball, Felicia J. Lee, Lesley Levy, Sarah Mart, Lee Mintz, Brian Morehouse, Shirley O'Neil, Laura W. Perna, Densil R.R. Porteous II, Ray P.R. Quirolgico, Lorrie Ranck, Alyson Solomon, Rameen Talesh, Barbara Thomas, and Linda L. Thomas Worthy all helped out in one way or another, and I am grateful for their assistance.

Additionally, it's hard enough to try things out on your own as a student, much less agree to be featured in a book about how you struggled and then found success. Many thanks to the current students and recent graduates who contributed their insightful tips and approaches to dealing with stress: Christina Bacock, Sherra Bennett, Sriya Bhumi, Ryinta Brown, Rebecca Kopilovitch, Stacy Serrano, Chris Stockton,

Nihar Suthar, Josh Swedlund, Junior Vancea, and Sara Smits Wilson. I appreciate the trust and faith you put in me when sharing your stories.

I also owe some public appreciation to everyone who helped me during my journey as an educator, a writer, and a student. Thank you to the countless teachers and professors over the years who encouraged me to write, and to the college students I've worked with who most often ended up teaching me more than I taught them.

I am exceptionally fortunate to have a remarkable support system of friends and family who helped me along the way. Much love and appreciation to Nicole Cortez, Emily Elliott, and Matthew Warren for being the best of friends despite my ridiculousness. My parents, Peter and Joan; sister Shannon; and brother Buud (okay fine, "Peter") definitely deserve much thanks and appreciation for being such loving and supportive cheerleaders during this project—and throughout my life. My in-laws, too, are the best possible folks I could imagine, and I'm grateful for all of their interest and support of this endeavor.

Some younger folks deserve a bit of recognition as well. To my beloved kiddos, who help me keep such wonderful perspective of what's worth stressing over and what's not. I love you both so much and am so honored to be your mom! And to Griffin, who adds so much to our little family.

Lastly, to David, the love of my life and my absolute dearest friend. Thank you for being so supportive of my writing, whether it be by helping me talk through ideas or by cooking dinner or by bringing home flowers when I'm struggling to balance my own stress. I know you did countless little tasks and absorbed endless responsibilities that I never saw while I was working on this book, and I thank you for giving me that luxury. Meeting you really was the best thing that's ever happened to me, and I look forward to many more milestones together.

Kelci Lynn Lucier

Introduction

When you imagined your life in college, you probably pictured some basic scenes: Classrooms with professors and attentive students. Living in a residence hall or apartment with other people. A fun social scene. Hanging out in the quad on a warm day. You were also probably excited about the ability to make your own choices about where to go, what you wanted to do, and with whom you wanted to spend your time.

While you will find all of those things within the college experience, they take place within a relatively stressful context. You and your classmates might need to be that attentive in class because the professor moves so quickly through the material. You might enjoy living in your residence hall, but you and your roommate aren't getting along too well. You might love hanging out in the quad, but you're struggling to find a balance between your need to get things done and your desire to relax every once in a while. And while you're grateful for the independence and the freedom to make your own choices about nearly every detail of your college life, that kind of open decision-making can sometimes feel overwhelming.

There's no way around it: College is stressful.

You don't have to be stressed, however, just because you're in a stressful environment. The key is learning how to soar through the stressors of college without becoming a stressed-out, burned-out mess.

This book will help you learn how to navigate successfully through the common stresses of college life, whether it's your first semester in college or your last. The goal of the book is to help you identify and deal with stress as you focus on the rest of your college life and, ultimately, graduating. You can read it cover to cover before you ever step foot in a college lecture hall, or you can keep it on your shelf and refer to it as needed.

Because there are so many different aspects of college stress, the material is broken down by topic. Feeling stressed over a bad professor, for example, is a very different kind of experience than feeling stressed over a bad roommate. Additionally, the ways to deal with various kinds of stress will depend on the specifics of the situation.

Each chapter deals with a type of stress that you may encounter during your time in school. You'll be presented with five questions about each stress-related topic that can help you identify the sources and factors of a particular kind of stress. You'll then find a multitude of solutions, broken down further for specific circumstances.

While I was doing interviews and research for this book, I lost count of how many people said, "I wish I had something like this when I was in college!" Professors said it, students said it, administrators said it. Encountering and dealing with stress during one's college years is very much a shared experience—for good and bad.

College, after all, can be one of the best times of your life. And while stress will undoubtedly be part of your college experience, this book will help you learn how to make it a manageable aspect instead of something that completely overwhelms you. Finding the sources of your stress, confronting them, and coming up with approaches to prevent them from resurfacing whenever possible are skills that can help you focus on the more enjoyable parts of being in school. Ideally, with your stress under control, you'll be able to stay on track to graduate, grow and learn as much as possible along the way, and toss your cap with pride—instead of relief—on graduation day.

CHAPTER 1

Academic Stress

The main goal of attending college is, of course, to earn a degree. Consequently, doing well in your classes should most often be your highest priority. Knowing that your schoolwork is most important can help you prioritize the stressors you face—but it can also add stress to an already stressful situation. After all, the academic and intellectual challenges of college are much different from high school. The stakes are higher for each assignment, and passing some classes can depend on your performance on a single exam, lab report, presentation, or paper. College courses often require different and more advanced study skills, the ability to work collaboratively on group projects, and excellent time management. But how can you make your academics the most important thing on your to-do list without also making them the most stressful? Fortunately, doing so might be easier than you think—with a few smart approaches, of course.

Academic Stress: Identifying the Sources

The most critical—and most helpful—step to take when dealing with academic stress is to figure out the source of that stress. If you've been in college for a while, try to remember the exact areas that have caused the most stress in your academic life so far. If you're just starting college, think back to your high school years. When and in which subjects did you struggle the most? (Even if you've been a top-notch student, you've undoubtedly had some ups and downs in your academic career.)

It can be very easy to feel stressed-out about your classes without really understanding what that means or where, specifically, that stress is coming from. Do you struggle with study skills? With writing? With reading comprehension? With group work? With test anxiety? With leaving things to the last minute? Spend some time thinking seriously about what makes you the most stressed when it comes to your academic responsibilities. As you work to identify the main sources of stress in your academic life, consider the following questions:

Academic Stress: The Five Questions

1. *What academic requirements must I meet this semester?* Determine what your most basic goals are. Do you have to earn a certain GPA to keep your scholarship? Do you need to carry a certain amount of units to keep your status as a full-time student? Do you need to pass the first in a series of courses (for example: Chemistry 101 so you can take Chemistry 102 next semester) to stay on track academically? Do you need to complete certain general education requirements (like a foreign language) by the time this academic year is over?

2. *What would my ideal academic performance be this semester?* Is it important for you to earn straight As? To get As in the courses required for your major? To pass your science requirement? To get to know a specific professor so that you can approach him or her about doing research this summer? To improve your GPA by a certain amount?

3. *What is a reasonable academic goal for me to set this semester?* Is it realistic to aim for straight As, or is that going to cause you unnecessary stress? What kind of academic performance

will you be happy with? What can you reasonably aim for given your own academic strengths, weaknesses, and previous performances?

4. *What resources can I use to help me meet my goals?* Have you been part of a study group in the past that worked well (and productively) together? Do you know students in some of your classes with whom you can partner early in the semester? Have your professors recommended external texts, websites, or other resources that can help supplement the required course materials? What materials can you utilize from previous classes that might help you with this semester? What offices on campus can help you if, for example, you need help with a paper or with learning some additional study skills? What people can provide individual support? What networks can you tap into that can help you deal with academic stress?

5. *How will I know when I should ask for help?* What in the past have been indicators that you are falling behind? Not understanding the material? Not studying well for an upcoming exam? What are the signs for when you are starting to feel overwhelmed? How do you normally approach a situation when you are having trouble academically? What kinds of grades do you need to watch out for that will indicate your need to ask for assistance of some kind?

Finding Solutions

Once you've identified the exact sources of your stress, it's much easier to find solutions for each one. As you think about your answers to the questions you just asked yourself, themes will probably arise. Once you've highlighted a particular stressor as a key one, you can break down your stress into parts and find ways to avoid or resolve each part.

Solution #1: Talk with Your Professors

Fortunately, your professors can be some of your best allies when it comes to preventing and dealing with academic stress during your time in school. Unfortunately, however, professors can also be intimidating if you aren't sure how or when to approach them for help.

Try to keep in mind that your professors were once college students, too. They likely needed help, struggled with certain classes, were frustrated with group project assignments, and had general questions about course requirements, grades, and exam preparation—just like you do. Professors help their students learn; they want you to be successful. To that end, they expect to interact with students regularly, to answer questions, and to solve problems.

Planning Your Meeting

It's perfectly understandable to feel intimidated by someone who is incredibly smart and partly in control of your success in a class. Don't let that discomfort stop you from asking for help, though. In a college environment, one of your responsibilities as a student is to seek out resources when you need them. And your professors can be a great asset for dealing with academic stress, whether it's being proactive and helping you do well on an upcoming exam or being reactive and helping you understand why you did so poorly. You might be pleasantly surprised at the reaction you get.

If you aren't sure where to start, follow these steps:

1. Check to see when your professor has office hours; he or she will usually post them online, outside his or her office door, or even on the course syllabus. To set up a time to talk, you can send an e-mail, call, or even ask in person after class.

2. Talk with other students about what your professors are like outside of class. The professor you find incredibly intimidating just might be the friendliest person imaginable when he or she is not in class. Conversely, it would be good to know that your seemingly low-key professor prefers if students come to office hours with a specific list of questions or concerns.

3. If you aren't sure exactly what to say during your meeting, use the five questions mentioned at the beginning of this chapter as a springboard for topics. Write down two or three key points that you want to bring up.

4. When it's time for your meeting, arrive a few minutes early. Make sure to introduce yourself, say what class you're in, and describe why you want to meet. Professors meet with students for a wide range of reasons, so identifying why you're there will help focus the conversation.

Specific Topics to Discuss

When you want to meet with your professor for academic reasons, your questions will usually fall into one of two camps: a particular concept you don't understand, or a specific assignment you're working on. Here's how to handle those two common situations:

- If you're struggling with some of the course material, be honest about what's hard for you. You undoubtedly are not the first person to struggle with a complicated concept, and your professor will ideally have some tips for helping you better master the material. Additionally, he or she might be able to explain things in a different way than what's allowable during class. If, for example, you learn best by asking many questions, office hours can provide that opportunity, whereas an hour-long class lecture with hundreds of students cannot.

- If you're struggling with an upcoming assignment, ask for guidance with your specific problem. Is it finding source material? Is it narrowing a broad topic? Is it understanding the assignment itself? It's okay to ask what your professor is looking for ahead of time—that helps you direct your efforts most efficiently. If you're starting to work on an upcoming paper, for example, you can ask your professor to review your thesis statement in advance. That way, you can make sure you're clear on the assignment and headed down the right path before you put too much time into your research. The last thing you need is to add more stress to your life because you wrote a great paper that failed to answer the actual prompt.

Solution #2: Handle a Problematic Class

Unfortunately, even if your professors all seemed reasonable, friendly, and skilled during the first week of classes, problems will inevitably pop up during your time in school. The professor everyone seems to love might seem horrible at explaining complicated concepts, while another might seem unfriendly and hostile to student questions.

If you have a professor or are in a course that you think is not a good fit, you have some options.

Drop the Class

If you still have time, and this course is not a required one for your major or graduation, you could consider the easiest solution: dropping the class. Dropping a class doesn't necessarily mean you did anything wrong; it just means the class wasn't right for you at the time.

Before dropping, however, make sure you are aware of what the consequences will be—both financially and academically. If you're thinking of dropping a class, make sure to meet with your academic adviser as soon as possible. You'll need his or her approval anyway, and your appointment can be a smart way for you to check in, discuss the situation, and brainstorm your options.

Switching Instead of Dropping

Before dropping a course, see if you can switch to take the same class with a different professor. Additionally, see if you can switch to a different teaching assistant (TA). Your professor might be moving too fast during lecture, but a great TA can utilize your seminar time to help everyone better understand the material.

Determine the Source of the Problem

If it's too late to drop the class, you can't or don't want to drop the class, or you're otherwise just stuck with a "bad" professor, it's time to think about what exactly makes this particular class such a challenge for you.

- **Presentation of material:** If your professor moves through the material too quickly or doesn't present it well, think creatively about how you can learn what you need to know. Can you form a study group? Spend more time reading the course materials and going over the lecture notes outside of class? Break up each chapter with some friends so that everyone focuses on one particular concept and then explains it to the rest of the group each week? While your professor is certainly the main resource for the material, he or she is not the *only* resource you have.

- **Your mastery of a subject:** If you are having problems mastering a concept, you can try to adjust your approach to the material. Perhaps just reading the textbook isn't going to cut it in this class and you'll need to do something else, like make an outline as you read or prepare flashcards that you can use for studying (and writing papers) later. Ask your friends in the class what they're doing. Do they read before the class lecture? After? Participate in online discussions when they have questions? Meet regularly for office hours?

- **Grading disagreements:** If you think your professor is an unfair grader, it might be time to adjust your expectations. Did you think your paper should have received an A but your professor thinks it earned a B? If so, try talking with your professor about what an A paper would have included. (Be careful, however, to make sure your meeting focuses on what to strive for in a future A-worthy paper instead of why your previous assignment should have met that standard. The point of a conversation like this is to help you better understand your professor's expectations, not to ask your professor to justify what grade he or she thought you earned.) Next time, be sure you're clear on what your professor is looking for in a specific assignment. No matter the context, if you're stuck with this professor and class, it might be time to step up—and adjust—your game so that you can succeed in your class instead of stress out about it.

- **Disagreement with a professor:** Lastly, if you find yourself in the unusual situation of having a professor you just don't agree with—say, in the way he or she analyzes a piece of literature or deconstructs a historical political movement—but whom you are also stuck with, do your best to learn what you can from the situation. In these kinds of circumstances, Professor Thomas L. Burkdall, Associate Professor of Writing and Rhetoric and Director of the Center for Academic Excellence at Occidental College in Los Angeles, encourages students "...to take up the professor's perspective for the term—even if you disagree, you may learn valuable lessons by seeing the topic from a new perspective." In essence: Don't let a bad or mismatched professor turn your required course into a stress-inducing experience. Instead, use the class as an opportunity to learn something new, shift your focus, and transform your stress into a learning tool.

✪ Straight from a Student: Handling a Tough Grader

Christina Bacock, a 2013 graduate of the University of Nevada, Reno, had a journalism professor her first year who was extremely harsh on her writing skills. Her professor's feedback and questioning of her capabilities left her "appalled and very hurt."

Bacock, however, wanted to pursue a career in journalism, so she kept her focus on her long-term goal despite her professor's criticism. Three years later, another journalism professor (who taught Bacock in a Magazine Writing course) was impressed enough with Bacock's writing that he later published one of her stories in a compilation of student writing.

These different experiences with professors helped Bacock realize that "not everyone is going to like my work...especially when it comes to writing." She learned to not immediately stress over specific criticisms, but instead to listen and "consider who was saying it, why they were saying it, and to remember what they have said in the past. This helped me reduce stress because I wasn't thinking of everyone anymore."

This approach also helped Bacock stay authentic to her work while learning when and how to process feedback. An added benefit, of course, is that Bacock learned how not to become so easily stressed-out as a result of one person's negative opinion. "Ultimately, I still stress a little bit because I want to be good at what I do, but I don't let it get to me," she says.

Solution #3: Be Clear on Your Professors' Expectations

Ever been in this scenario? You think you are going to own an upcoming midterm like a boss but then end up completely failing. What the heck just happened?

If you aren't clear on the expectations—from the beginning—in your classes, you're automatically setting yourself up for frustration, failure, and stress. The best intentions can lead you astray if all of your hard work isn't contributing to the right end result.

For example, you can spend a significant amount of time studying the lecture notes for a class only to realize too late that the midterm focused on the out-of-class reading, not the lecture material. Or you could have written an amazing essay that discussed the role of women in a particular novel when you were actually supposed to have discussed the role of one single female character in the novel. Did you work hard, put in effort, and do your best in these kinds of situations? Definitely. But you also may have failed the assignment.

Study the Syllabus

There are two great sources for making sure that you're clear on course expectations: the class syllabus and your professor. The syllabus is often handed out and/or made available online on the first day of classes. It describes the course, lists what readings need to be done prior to each class meeting, has a schedule for when and where the class meets and what each class's topic will be, and lists major assignments and their due dates.

Before you do anything else for a class, study the syllabus. Yes, you even have to study the syllabus! Follow this two-step approach:

1. Read through each syllabus casually the first time, just looking at the general tone and feel of the class. Is the reading load heavy? Are there lots of smaller assignments, or does your grade depend solely on a final exam? Are you expected to do things outside of class, like spend a few hours each week in a language lab?

2. After a day or two, go over each syllabus again. This time, mark down on your main calendar (wherever that is—your wall, your smartphone, your computer) every major assignment, their due dates, and reminders. Each class's midterms, for example, should be marked at least twice on your calendar: once on the actual day of the exam and once as a reminder the week before. You don't want to inadvertently sabotage all of your hard work by having a major assignment or exam sneak up on you. You are much more likely to put yourself in a

stressful situation if you think your statistical physics midterm is in "mid-March sometime" than if you are reminded in your calendar on March 5 that the midterm will be taking place one week later on March 12.

Ask Your Professor

In addition to your syllabi, your professors are the best source for making sure you are crystal clear on what will be expected of you. Take detailed notes whenever your professor discusses what is expected on an upcoming assignment. Make sure to flag or highlight anything your professor mentions will be on the next exam or final. Do your best to keep up with the reading and attend class on a regular basis so that you can always be mindful of what you'll need to pay most attention to. It's much less stressful—and much more productive—to think, "Okay, I really need to understand this as I'm reading it because it's going to be on the final" than it is to say to yourself, "Okay, I have to remember to focus on this later when I catch up on the reading this weekend. *If* I can get to it this weekend..."

Additionally, be clear on specifics. Some professors, for example, expect you to do some outside research on each paper you submit, whereas others simply want you to analyze a text yourself. Some professors expect you to cite often from a novel you are examining, whereas others find too many quotations to be filler. Even if you only touch base for a quick 10 minutes, make the effort to connect with your professors—during office hours, after class, or via e-mail—about what they are looking for in any major assignments or exams.

If you find yourself in a situation where you performed poorly because you failed to meet course expectations, you can still learn from the experience—even if you cannot change your grade. The lesson?

Know what's expected of you *beforehand*. Knowing what you'll need to do, how you'll need to perform, and when you'll be expected to do so can go a long way in helping to reduce, if not eliminate, academic-related stress.

Solution #4: Consider Study Groups

Study groups can be an amazing resource. They can help break up difficult assignments, help you better understand the materials, and even just offer a place to commiserate with others when things are particularly difficult.

How to Find or Create a Productive Group

Finding a good study group, however, is easier said than done. You'll need to consider the following factors:

1. How do you learn best? Do you learn best by talking in a quiet study room in the library, for example, or by talking loosely about the material in a busy campus coffee shop?
2. Do you learn best with just one or two people or with a large group? Which kinds of group dynamics are you most comfortable with?
3. What kinds of people do you learn best from? Are you, for example, an introvert who learns best from other introverts, or do you need an outgoing leader of the group? Remember to think about how you best learn, not necessarily what makes you the most comfortable. You might need to step a bit outside of your comfort zone if you're going to find your ideal study group arrangement.

Once you're clear on what kind of study group you want and need, think carefully about which students in your class would work well in that particular kind of group. Is one student you know great at remembering facts in ways that other students can learn from, whereas someone else excels at understanding and explaining concepts? A study group is not just about finding strong individuals; it's also about finding a group that is, in essence, larger than the sum of its parts. The individuals in your study group should all complement each other's strengths and weaknesses so that everyone contributes, shares, and benefits equally.

Keeping Study Groups Productive

Working with a study group is complicated. A study group comprising your friends may sound fantastic, but it might not be the most productive. Be clear with a study group that you're either forming or joining about what the expectations are. For example, you should hash out ahead of time:

- How often will you meet? For how long?
- What will you do for breaks? How long will those breaks be?
- Will people bring food?
- Will you rotate locations?

While your main function will be studying, it's also important to spend some time getting to know each other and setting some guidelines for how things will work. That way, when everyone is sick and cranky during midterms and finals, you'll have a structure to fall back on so that your study group becomes a source of strength instead of stress.

Additionally, what started out as a great study group may change as time goes on. You may have done such a great job connecting with your group members that the nature of the group has gone from academic to social. Or perhaps meetings stopped being effective for you because the course material shifted as the semester progressed—at first you needed to memorize facts, but now you're applying that knowledge to long essays or lab projects. At that point, it's time to take a hard look at what's actually going on during the study group.

Jeanette Duffels, MLIS, a librarian at the Southern California University of Health Sciences in Whittier, California, suggests asking yourself, "Are you goofing off more than studying? Do the other members of your group complement your learning style? Are you performing better in class than you would be if you studied alone?"

Study Groups Not Your Style?

Duffels also reminds students that, "It is perfectly fine to try a study group and decide that it is not for you." A study group, after all, should help you focus on homework and your classes, not add to your stress by misallocating your time. If you are learning fine on your own, don't feel obligated to join or stay in a study group that's just draining your precious time.

Solution #5: Keep Your Eye on Your Ultimate Goal—Graduation

It can be easy to become so lost in the trees of college life that you forget to see the larger forest. There are so many things going on all day, every day, that long-term goals seem both unattainable and too far away.

When it comes to keeping your stress in check, however, it's critical to keep your big-picture goals in mind. True, things can seem overwhelming more often than not, but reminding yourself why you're making the sacrifices you are is important.

Create Visual Reminders

One way to keep yourself focused on graduating is to remind yourself of that goal daily. Hang up a picture of your high school graduation so you can remember what it feels like to graduate after several years of hard work. Make a small bulletin board with a collage of images of what you'd like your life to be like after you graduate. Do you want to go to graduate school? Have a nice house? Live somewhere in particular? Have the freedom to travel? Be a teacher? A doctor? An entrepreneur? Support a family? Many of life's simple luxuries are made much easier if you have a college degree. Reminding yourself visually of where you'd like to be is an easy, motivating way to make sure you do what it takes to get yourself there.

Motivate Yourself

Another way to remind yourself of your goal to graduate is to place little motivators where you'll see—and need—them most. Some quick and inexpensive ideas include:

- Doing a quick Internet search for quotations about education that you can turn into a graphic and use as a background on your computer or tablet.
- Signing up for e-newsletters or following reputable Twitter accounts that provide you with weekly tips and motivation during your time in school.
- Meeting a friend for coffee at least once a month to discuss things that are going really well instead of things that are causing you stress.

- Hanging up a chart with all of your major assignments listed for the semester; as you finish each one, cross it off your list. Reward yourself along the way for doing well and for making it one step closer to graduation day.

A college degree is as valuable as it is because it takes a lot of determination and skill to earn. Try to remind yourself that having to work hard to earn your diploma is something to feel proud of—not stressed about.

Perspective Equals Less Stress

Keeping perspective—both short-term and long-term—can help reduce stress and keep your focus. When working with her students, Lorrie Ranck, MA, Dean of Learning Resources at De Anza College in Cupertino, California, likes "to engage in dialogues around the larger goals of their life and then how their academic goals are situated in the panoramic view. Graduation is a vista point but not the only one, and ultimately you get back in the car and keep traveling."

Solution #6: Learn How to Study at the College Level

Learning at the college level is likely an entirely new challenge, even if you were successful in high school. What got you by in high school may no longer cut it in college. Or the basic skills you mastered in high school need to be kicked up a notch for college-level material. Reading comprehension, writing, critical thinking, studying, and test-taking all take on new meanings in a college environment.

Give Yourself Some Time

One thing to remember—and not stress about—is that learning to perform academically at the college level takes time. It is an unreasonable expectation to think that you can go from high school to college without experiencing any academic hiccups or challenges. (In fact, for the 2011–2012 academic year, only 16.8 percent of all undergraduates earned "mostly As" in college, as reported by the U.S. Department of Education's National Center for Education Statistics.) Your classes are different, your exams are different, the material is different, the learning environment is different. So, naturally, your performance will be different. Realize that this is part of your education, not necessarily something to stress over.

That being said, of course, you do want to make sure you adapt to your college academic requirements as best and as quickly as possible. Learning "how to study" might seem basic, but it's critically important. Simply going to class and doing the reading may not be enough—you'll probably need to review the material more than once and in different ways in order to really learn it.

Find the Study Habits That Work Best for You

There's no magic answer for learning how to study at the college level. There is, however, a magic answer for you as an individual. What works for your friends and your roommate may not work for you, but there definitely is something out there that will click with your brain and how you learn—you just have to spend some time to try to find it.

When trying to figure out your own best way of studying at the college level, break the question down into two main parts: your external environment and your internal environment.

1. Think about the external environments that most help you learn. Do you like to ask questions and participate in class discussions? Do you like to sit back quietly during a class and let the information sink in? Do you do better in large lectures or in smaller seminars? Do you like to study and write when it's quiet or when there are people around you? If you could think of your ideal time, place, and method for studying, what would it be like?

2. Also think about the internal environment you need to help you learn. Does your mind need to be free from stress? Does your brain work better in the morning or late at night? Do you remember things better if you read them, listen to them, or interact with them? Will you retain more from your Introduction to Psychology textbook if you highlight as you read, take notes as you read, and/or listen to music as you read? Do you work best in short periods or over long stretches of time?

In order to truly develop college study skills, you have to first figure out what kind of learner you are. Once you know that, you can adapt your own methods to nearly any class.

Solution #7: Figure Out Where to Go for Help

If you find yourself struggling—and likely stressing—about your academics, rest assured that there are multiple resources on every college campus to help you. College is difficult, but it's not designed to fail everyone out. And you are not the first student to face some academic challenges along the way. So just where can you go for help?

1. **Course-specific help:** Think specifically about each class you're having a problem with. What resources can you tap into that cater specifically to that class? Can you meet with the professor? Join a study group of some friends who are in your same lecture section? Talk to your TA? Reread your textbook or course reader? Ask someone who has already taken the class for advice?

2. **Subject-matter help:** Second, think a little more broadly and look at where you can go for help on the general topic. What resources, for example, are available for students studying a foreign language? Are there supplemental materials you can use in the language lab? In the library? In a specific academic department? Are there tutors available on campus? If you're struggling with your Basic Web Design and Programming class, is there a computer science major in your fraternity or sorority who can help?

3. **Big-picture help:** What major offices on campus can help students who are having difficulty? Is there a peer tutoring or mentoring program you can join? Is there a cocurricular club of people interested in your major that can serve as a resource? Is there some kind of academic support center that specifically helps students learn study skills or test preparation? Is there a writing center that can help you figure out a thesis and review your drafts before you submit your final assignment? It's a rare college campus that doesn't offer some kind of institutional academic support—and a rare student who doesn't need to tap into those support systems at least once during his or her time in school.

Don't Wait!

More important than where you get help, however, is when. Professor Thomas L. Burkdall, Associate Professor of Writing and Rhetoric and Director of the Center for Academic Excellence at Occidental College in Los Angeles, strongly advises his students to reach out for help as soon as possible. "At the first sign of trouble, seek assistance. That may be when you are struggling with your first assignment or when you receive a grade that you were not expecting (and then it should be on an assignment or test worth a smaller portion of your grade). Don't be afraid or embarrassed to seek help!" The only thing to be embarrassed about, after all, is *not* asking for help when you needed it most.

Solution #8: Use the Library and Technological Services

Although sometimes underutilized, the library and technological services available on your campus can be great resources for dealing with your academic workload (and stress).

Befriend a Librarian

In addition to the physical space, libraries offer a unique resource: librarians. "Libraries offer a variety of resources for study help," notes Jeanette Duffels, MLIS, a librarian at the Southern California University of Health Sciences. "It is easy to look at a course syllabus and not think beyond the required textbook, but librarians spend a lot of time figuring out what books, videos, models, and other items can help students learn." If you're struggling to understand the material, a librarian can be an excellent resource for helping you find other ways to engage with the content and retain what you need to know.

Don't be shy about approaching a librarian, either; they're there to help. As Duffels notes, "Here's a secret that should be obvious: librarians love to help people. You can ask a librarian for help in person, over the phone, through e-mail, or sometimes via instant message. If they don't have an answer, they will find out who does. Often we look busy, but we are never too busy to help you, so politely interrupt us."

Use Technology to Your Academic Advantage

Many, if not most, of your professors and courses will incorporate technology into the classroom. What used to be taught by lecture notes is now delivered via PowerPoint presentation, online forums, Twitter conversations, and Facebook discussion groups. You may be tempted only to interact in online forums as often as the course requires—or you may be tempted to use social media only for your social life. Realize, however, that technology and your campus technological services are primarily designed to help facilitate your learning. Instead of viewing a class's online posts and tweets as obligatory, try viewing them as a resource. If you're struggling with a concept, ask how other students are approaching it. If you're not clear about an example presented in the reading, ask for clarification.

If you're worried that your professor might see you as someone struggling with the material, this is likely not the case. Instead, your professor might see you as someone interested in learning, as someone brave enough to ask for more information, and as a key contributor to class discussion—both in the classroom and in virtual discussion forums.

Solution #9: Ask for Assistance with a Learning Disability, Disorder, or Difference

College presents unique challenges to students who have learning disabilities, learning disorders, and/or learning differences (LDs). If you are one of these students, you should connect with your college as soon as possible. Whether or not you utilized services for students with LDs at any other time during your education, be sure you do so in college. And that means speaking with people as soon as you decide where you're going to school.

You may have mentioned your LD on your college application, but that information may not have been communicated to the people who can help you. Or you may have mentioned it to your academic adviser during orientation, but he or she needs an official notification from a campus academic support center. Your best bet is to proactively connect with the people and offices that will need to know about your LD.

If you aren't sure where to start, head to the dean of students office, a learning center, or your academic adviser to discuss the particulars of your situation. You might, for example, need to present documentation about your LD or even take additional tests so that your school can determine how best to assist you.

While it doesn't matter *where* you start, it does matter *when*. Going to an academic support center a few days before your final exams is too late. (Although it should be noted that it's better to go late than not at all.) Whether it's the summer before classes begin, during orientation week, or even during the first week or two of classes, you need to connect as soon as you possibly can. Forming a strong, immediate connection with the services you need as a learner should be at the top of your priority list.

How your campus meets your LD needs depends on what your school is reasonably able to provide. Make sure you have access to the support you need before you need it. Even if you don't utilize the services right away, you'll at least have them available when and where you do end up needing some assistance.

Solution #10: Develop Tips for Handling Stress During High-Stress Periods

While everyday life in college has its highs and lows, there are particular times when things become especially stressful. Midterm weeks and finals, for example, present challenges to even the most organized, efficient, normally stress-free student. So what can you do when things are looking even more overwhelming than usual?

Break Down Stress Into Chunks

One thing to keep in mind is that the highest-stress periods of a college semester are usually very short in duration. While you may be stressing a bit in advance, your midterm or final exam is really only going to take a few hours. Consequently, it's important to break down the source(s) of high-stress periods into more manageable chunks.

Take that midterm exam, for example. You'll probably be tested a bit on the outside-of-class reading, on the material covered in class, and on your general understanding of key concepts and ideas. Have you stayed on top of the reading? If not, how far behind are you? If so, what techniques (for example: highlighting) did you use so that you could review the material later? Break down the reading into manageable chunks for review, and do so far enough in advance that you'll be able to re-familiarize yourself with the material without having to cram.

You can use a similar approach to the material covered in class lectures. What do you think is the most important? Do you have notes you can use? What concepts are you the most and the least comfortable with? Look at your calendar and decide how much you need to review each day in advance of your exam, and then break the material down accordingly.

Plan in Advance

Planning in advance is equally important—if not more so—when dealing with large research projects. When looking at high-stress periods, take a deep breath and remember that short-term stress can be mitigated by longer-term planning. If you tend to worry and get stressed-out thinking, "I have a midterm in two weeks and I don't feel prepared," make a plan. Then, you can genuinely reassure yourself by saying, "I have a midterm in two weeks. I have the material broken down so that, if I study thirty minutes a day in advance of the exam, I will be in great shape." And then make it happen! Easier said than done, sure—but mastering study skills is part of college life.

Solution #11: Master Time Management

One of the biggest challenges—and sources of academic stress—for college students is time management. Sometimes, it seems that unless you can bend the space-time continuum, you simply won't be able to get all of your academic work done by your deadlines.

Here's a secret: Time management in college does not mean getting everything done exactly when and how you wanted it. Time management means learning how to prioritize.

Create a Time Management System

One key factor of time management is having some kind of system to manage your schedule. It's a rare (if not nonexistent) student who can graduate from college without using some kind of calendar to keep track of things. There are countless options available—online, on your smartphone, on your computer, on a tablet, in the cloud, or even on traditional paper printouts—for college students in particular. How you plan your time is not as important as the simple act of doing so. Use your time management system as a way to know exactly where your time is going and plan it accordingly. Ideally, it will help you manage your energy, involvement, coursework—and stress levels.

Reading Assignments

Long reading assignments often require a significant block of time in your schedule. To manage the load but still keep up with your classwork, prioritize based on time—and content. "You do not have to achieve excellence on every assignment, nor in every course," advises Professor Thomas L. Burkdall, Associate Professor of Writing and Rhetoric and Director of the Center for Academic Excellence at Occidental College in Los Angeles. "Allow yourself to do well enough in some courses, on some assignments, and focus your energies on others. You don't always need to read every word of every text, either—but make choices based on experience with a course, discipline, or professor; don't just guess!" For example, if you're struggling with an economics class, be sure you prioritize that reading over your history class's—especially if you're already somewhat familiar with the time period being discussed in history. If you're not going to read an assignment thoroughly, at least skim the material so that you can generally understand the class discussion and then return to the reading later if time permits.

You can also consider breaking down a heavy reading assignment between classmates or a study group. Each person can be responsible for, say, fifty pages of a large chapter. When you get together as a group, each person can provide a summary and outline of their assigned section, leaving all group members with detailed information about the chapter as a whole.

✪ Straight from a Student: Time Management

Rebecca Kopilovitch, a senior at the University of San Francisco, manages her time by being vigilant about staying on top of her coursework. Getting her academic work done as soon as possible helps her handle her stress. "I get my work done immediately so I can actually relax," she says. "I don't mind studying at night; I actually like it because there is no time limit. I can study as much or as little as I want...Once I do my work, or everything I could to complete/prepare for class, stress goes away."

This time management approach also helps Kopilovitch deal with higher-stress periods like exam time. "The morning of a test I am usually already at a calm state of mind because everything that was under my control was either done or not done ahead of time," she notes. "I'm mostly stressed when I know I have something to do about it; I never want to be the one to say 'could have, should have, would have...'"

Limit Outside Activities If Necessary

Time management can also mean learning to say no to nonacademic commitments. Your priority in college is to graduate, plain and simple. So when things become particularly stressful, refocus on your ultimate goal and go from there. Yes, you may have agreed to serve on the planning committee for a large, upcoming campus event, but if your academic performance is starting to suffer, it's time to gracefully withdraw. Don't feel bad for saying no to requests from others about your involvement or commitments to nonacademic projects. In contrast, you *should* feel bad for breaking your commitment to yourself to succeed in—and graduate from—college. While it can be challenging, good time management involves knowing when to step aside or become less involved.

Again—Lean on Your Campus Resources

Lastly, time management also means learning to utilize the resources available to you. Students who go to a writing center on campus, for example, aren't necessarily doing so because they're bad writers. They might be doing so because they are excellent writers. If your time is limited, it makes a lot more sense to make sure you're using your time wisely. If visiting a writing center can help you narrow down your thesis, stay on target, and avoid unnecessary drafts, revisions, and time spent just starting at a blank screen, then you're using your time wisely. Similarly, meeting with a professor, finding a study group, talking with your TA, and otherwise reaching out for assistance can be great time savers—and, consequently, stress reducers.

Solution #12: Don't Stress over What Can't Be Changed

Even though you may be much more in control of your life in college than in high school, quite a bit of it is still out of your hands. The amazing paper you spent forever on apparently wasn't up to your professor's standards. You suspect that your professors secretly got together and planned their syllabi so that all four of your midterms are in the same week. Or you simply have classes with very heavy reading loads that won't let up until after the semester ends.

A Common Culprit: Grades

Just like the other areas of your college experience, there are some things related to your college academics that warrant some stress and concern—and others that you just have to make yourself not stress over. You can't change the way your professors grade, for example, so trying to argue your grade, getting upset about your grade, or losing sleep over your grade are only going to add to your stress load. In contrast, learning what you should do for the next paper, planning your paper in advance, and approaching the new assignment with a positive attitude can greatly reduce your stress.

Remember, too, that earning grades that are lower than what you had hoped for or expected doesn't have to be a bad thing. For example:

- You might have fallen so in love with a new course that you didn't spend as much time as usual on a course you felt obligated to take.
- You learned that your career in biology might need to be reconsidered given your clumsiness—and boredom—in the lab.
- Sometimes, a high or low grade is, in fact, a very poor indicator of whether or not you learned anything. Passing your ridiculously difficult statistics class with a C might be your proudest academic achievement during your time in college; conversely, you might look back at the A you earned in Creative Writing and not feel particularly proud since you never felt challenged in the course.

Plan, Plan, Plan

Since you can't change the fact that you have four midterms all in one week or very heavy reading assignments between now and the end of the term, instead, figure out what you can do about them. Perhaps you can:

- Plan in advance when you're going to study for your midterms so that midterms week is a steady, thoughtful affair instead of a sleep-deprived, all-nighter stress fest.

- Break down your reading load into smaller chunks, including giving your brain a day off from reading each week so you can stay mentally sharp.
- Stay on top of your reading so that preparing for the midterm is calmer and less stress inducing than it has been in the past.

In essence, if something can't be changed, accept things as they are and make a plan to prepare. Stressing over the unchangeable only leads to more stress.

Solution #13: Undeclared Major? Celebrate It!

Are you stressed-out because you aren't sure what your major is or because you're thinking of switching? Give yourself a pat on the back. Yes, that's right—not declaring a major before you are required to frees you up for some unique, stress-free learning opportunities in college.

Many students feel pressure (which can often fester into stress) about having an undecided major. In reality, however, not declaring a major can alleviate academic stress instead of adding to it. You might be at liberty to take more diverse courses than you would if you were already aligned with a particular academic department. You might be more open to falling in love with a new subject or career path—one that you may not have considered if you had already declared a major.

View not having a declared major as a reason to relax. You have a unique opportunity to find out what interests you the most and to explore what most satisfies your mind and your heart. Your job as a college student is to learn all kinds of things—both inside and outside of the classroom. True, you have academic requirements, like passing your classes and making sure to take all of your general education classes. But you also have other requirements, like learning more about yourself as a scholar (yes, you're a scholar!) and as a learner. Your job is to let your mind explore, discover new things, and consider new ideas in ways you haven't before.

Consequently, not having a major can be a great way to facilitate this learning process. Save your stress for the things that matter more and let yourself enjoy your undeclared status for what it is: something to relax into and enjoy, not something to worry or feel pressure about.

Academic Stress: Conclusion and Highlights

Your actual coursework will probably be one of the biggest sources of stress during your time in college. With proactive planning, a willingness to ask for help, and some insight into your own academic strengths and weakness, however, you can work to transform your academic stress into your academic accomplishments.

- **Set reasonable, realistic academic goals for yourself.** Before each semester begins, think carefully and purposefully about what your academic goals are for each class and for the semester in general. Having specific academic goals in mind can help keep you focused, can help keep you motivated, and can help keep things in perspective.
- **Remember your ultimate college goal: graduation.** It can be easy to become stressed about minor things during your time in school. It can do your mind—and your stress levels—quite a bit of good to remind yourself of the benefits of having a college degree and of what you'll need to do to make that happen.
- **Be patient as you adjust to learning in a college environment.** Remember, too, that your adjustment is an ongoing process, not just

something that can be done in a few weeks. Whether it's learning how to study or declaring your major, your college education will be a constant work-in-progress. Be patient with yourself as you grow and learn instead of being frustrated and stressed-out over how much you still don't know.

- **Manage your time wisely.** One of the best ways to prevent, combat, and reduce college academic stress is to be the master of your time. Be mindful of how you're spending it, where you're spending it, and with whom you're spending it. If you're stressed about your academics, clear your schedule so you have the time you need to do well in your classes. Your time in college is highly valuable and needs to be allocated smartly.

- **Know where to go for help—and then go there.** It's an unrealistic and unfair expectation to put on yourself if you think you can make it through college without some kind of support. Know how to connect with your professors, TAs, tutors, mentors, peer advisers, learning centers, writing centers, study groups, librarians, and any and all other academic support systems on your campus. It's never too late to ask for help, and there's rarely, if ever, a reason not to. Utilize what's available on your campus as often and as much as possible.

CHAPTER 2

Financial Stress

Whether you're managing your money on your own for the first time or you consider yourself an old pro, the details of your financial life in college can quickly become overwhelming. With expenses that are both large and constant, staying on top of your finances becomes important not only for your financial health but also for your stress management.

It can be easy to feel so smothered by the cost of your education that paying attention to small financial decisions seems insignificant. And it can be easy to disassociate yourself from the large amounts of debt you're possibly accumulating; signing paperwork in the financial aid office, after all, can often feel more like a meaningless formality than a long-term agreement. In reality, however, you are investing heavily in your education—with money, work, time, and effort—and staying on top of your finances is a critical element of your college success.

Financial Stress: Identifying the Sources

When it comes to identifying the sources of your college financial stress, it might seem easier to try to think about what doesn't stress you out about money instead of what does. Ideally, however, your finances can provide you with a feeling of security and calm instead of anxiety and worry.

When trying to figure out the sources of your financial stress, it's important to remember that your financial life in college does not exist within a bubble. The choices you make now will affect your financial life after school, just like the choices you made before you came to college affect your life in school. And while this might seem overwhelming, it's more of a way to keep perspective and help you identify what is causing you the most stress—and why.

Financial Stress: The Five Questions

1. *What are my expenses this semester?* What do you need to pay for tuition? For room and board? For food? For fees? For car insurance, a car payment, gas, a parking pass, a bus pass, a bike permit, new tires? For other transportation, like a flight home? For clothes, for shoes, for jackets, for curtains for your new apartment, for printer paper? For electronics, for books, for course materials, for course fees, for software, for tutoring? For your cell phone? For utilities?

2. *When are these expenses due?* When are your biggest expenses due? Are there months that are much more expensive than others? What expenses absolutely must be met? What expenses might you be able to cut out during months when your money is tight? What expenses are smaller? When are they due?

3. *What are my sources of income?* If you are taking out loans, what do you need to do for them to be processed? What paperwork or other documentation (like your parents' tax forms or a financial aid form) will you need? If you are paying your own way, where will you be getting the money? What scholarships, grants, or other income sources do you have? If you're a first-year student, what have you been offered in your financial aid

package? What will you accept, decline, or look elsewhere for? If you're a returning student, how does your financial aid package compare to last year's package? How will you make up any new gaps, if there are any?

4. *When do my sources of income become available?* If you are receiving student loans, when will you actually get the money? How does this compare to when your major and minor expenses become due? Will you, for example, receive your loan in time to buy books before your classes begin? Will you receive your money in one lump sum (like a loan) or will you receive it throughout the year (like a paycheck)? When do you need to submit paperwork or other documentation so that you receive your money in time for your upcoming expenses?

5. *Where can I go if I find myself in a financial emergency?* If there is a large, unexpected expense, where can you go for additional funds? What people, organizations, banks, or other resources do you know that can help you? What resources have been made available to you that you might not have considered or looked into yet? What resources does your school have? What resources does your hometown have? What resources do your family, friends, religious community, professional community, Greek community, and other support systems have to offer if you find yourself in unexpected need?

Finding Solutions

There are an unlimited number of financial arrangements you might find yourself in—and thus, there are seemingly unlimited sources of financial stress. You might be paying for your entire college experience, right down to the last textbook; you might have financial help from another source, such as scholarships or your parents. While this book can't possibly touch on every scenario, it can provide techniques for managing financial stress that are universal.

Solution #1: Create a Budget

If you're going to manage your money and remain financially stress-free during your time in college, you're going to need a budget.

Unfortunately, even the term "budget" can cause people's stress levels to rise. Fortunately, however, this association doesn't always have to be the case. "Having a budget" and "budgeting" simply mean having a plan—and sticking to it.

Think of budgeting, then, more as a way to just make sure your money goes where it's supposed to go during your time in school. Budgeting doesn't have to involve all kinds of graphs and charts and ridiculous details and work. It simply involves having a system of your choice in place so that you:

1. Know where your money needs to go.
2. Make sure you have enough money to cover your costs.
3. Get your money where it needs to go when it needs to go there.

Where to Start

Begin with the basics. Before you start classes, make a list of all of your expenses. (If you're not sure where to start, try answering the five questions mentioned at the beginning of this chapter.) Try to group your expenses by topic and keep things relatively simple. Think about your average day in college from the moment you wake up until the moment you go to sleep. How are you paying for your housing? How are you paying for your bed? For your sheets? For your pajamas? For your breakfast? For your bicycle, car, backpack, classes, lunch, coffee, laptop, cell phone, running shoes, cable bill, Internet access? If you're not sure what your expenses are, just think about what you'll do during the day. Nearly every action you take—from sleeping and eating to studying and commuting—takes financial resources to accomplish. The first step of a budget, then, is figuring out what resources you're using in your college life.

Start Early

Try to make sure you have a budget before you begin college. Since making a budget and knowing where your money needs to go are things you can control and manage, the earlier you start, the better. Once you have your list, you'll need to determine how much these resources cost. What are your housing expenses? Food expenses? Personal expenses? Commuting expenses? Expenses directly related to your classes, like software, course readers, and lab fees? After you have specific amounts for how much certain parts of your life cost, you can figure out what you'll need to bring in each month to make sure those expenses are met.

What to Do with Your Lists

Actually making a budget is the final step in this process. Using your lists, make a monthly budget where you write down each month's expenses and the total amount of money that you'll need to meet these costs.

That final number is the amount of money you'll need to make sure you have available each month. Compare that to the amount of money you'll have available at that time, and you'll know if you're in the clear for that month. If not, you'll need to find additional sources of income—a job, a loan, a scholarship—or you'll need to look at where you can cut your expenses.

Solution #2: Track Your Spending

Knowing how much your expenses are and how much money you can spend doesn't necessarily mean you know how much you are actually spending at any given point in time. Having a budget won't work if you don't stay on top of where your money goes and aren't sure what your financial status is most of the time. After all, a budget is supposed to help reduce your college financial stress, not add to it.

Since you likely use a debit and/or credit card, it's easy to feel like you're not really spending money, as you rarely see cash. That makes it all the more important to track what you're spending. (Conversely, it also makes tracking easier, as your transactions are likely automatically documented online.) It can be incredibly stressful, especially at the end of a long semester, to worry and wonder if you will have enough money for rent, food, and other basics—not to mention costs you weren't planning on. If you've stayed on top of and on track with your budget, however, you can rest assured that your finances are one thing you don't have to stress about. At any given point in time, you'll know where your money has gone, how much you have available, and where the rest needs to go.

Try Online Banking

The biggest tool you can use to stay on top of your spending is to utilize some kind of tracking system. Most likely, you have online access to your bank account; from there, you can utilize tools your bank provides or other online resources to track your spending. You can see how much you're spending each month, what you're spending your money on, if you're sticking to your budget, and how much you have left until the end of the month. Even if your expenses are small in size and number, it's still important to keep track. Just one out-of-budget purchase can throw your finances out of balance and cause significant—and avoidable—stress.

Other Tracking Options

If online banking doesn't work for you, consider other methods. You can try a spreadsheet program, a financial software program, or an app for your smartphone. You can even use old-fashioned paper and a pen if that's what works best. It doesn't matter what you use, but it does matter that you use something. Keeping track of your spending does not have to be a complicated, annoying task. In fact, if you find a tracking method that works for you, staying on top of your budget should only take a few minutes each week.

Solution #3: Communicate Effectively with the Financial Aid Office

It's a rare student who never has to interact with the financial aid office during his or her time in school. By the end of their college careers, most students spend a great deal of time coordinating things with the financial aid staff. Consequently, being on good terms with the office and the people there is an important part of reducing your financial stress.

Densil R.R. Porteous II, Director of Admissions at the Columbus College of Art & Design in Ohio, states that "The key to working with any financial aid office is to be as transparent as possible during the process and to be patient." Patience and transparency can be difficult, but you'll need both no matter where you go to school. "Transparency is important because a financial aid office may not know what the circumstances are at home for you and your family— and sometimes they are able to take a deeper look into the aid they are offering if they are aware of extra places where family income may be going."

If possible, see if you can meet with the same financial aid staff member whenever you go in for an appointment, send an e-mail, or call on the phone. It can be helpful to always communicate with one person who is familiar with your particular situation. At some institutions, however, working with the same person isn't always an option.

Regardless of whom you're working with, there are a few simple rules to keep things running smoothly. Just like any other professional relationship, you want to keep things positive and respectful. As such, it's important to understand that financial aid professionals are very busy— particularly at peak times of the year—and deal with a large number of students and parents on a regular basis. Imagine how stressful your job would be if you had to handle the financial situation of hundreds, if not thousands, of students!

One thing you can do to help your situation is to always submit your required paperwork as soon as possible. Additionally, keep copies of everything you submit. That way, if something inadvertently gets lost, you can easily reproduce it. Even better than meeting the deadlines is getting things in *before* the deadline (whenever possible, of course). You'll likely beat the rush and, in some cases, get closer to the front of the line when it comes to aid disbursement.

✪ Straight from a Student: Financial Aid

Sherra Bennett, a 2013 graduate from the University of Michigan, Dearborn, was smart about her financial situation during her time in school. She created a budget, had a campus job, actively sought out scholarships, kept her grades in check, and got to know her financial aid advisers. She recalls that, "One of the first things I did was get to know and become friendly with the financial aid office," she says. "This made a huge difference in terms of getting business handled and being able to have problems resolved quickly if they arose. The financial aid office was also able to assist in telling me the best times to apply/have everything submitted in order to receive more Pell Grants (a.k.a. free money)."

Sure, the financial aid office might seem intimidating, but think of it like this: There is a significant chance that if you treat the staff respectfully, explain your situation, and are proactive about your options, you will be compensated for your work. Intentionally establishing a good relationship with the financial aid staff can be one of the smartest choices you make during your college years.

After all, financial aid is stressful enough when everything runs smoothly. There are loan papers to sign, campus jobs to find, deposits and checks to coordinate, and all kinds of details that pop up no matter how well you plan. Because of this, staying on top of your financial aid can greatly reduce the stress of your college financial life. Financial problems can frequently originate from problems with financial aid, so being proactive, respectful, and patient with the financial aid office can help reduce problems at their source. Some stresses in college can't be avoided, but a basic effort to stay on top of your financial aid is one of the smartest steps you can take to prevent unnecessary financial stress.

Solution #4: Reassure Yourself That College Is Still a Good Investment

Sometimes, when your stress level is at its highest and your bank account is at its lowest, you might find yourself wondering if college is still a good investment. A college degree, after all, doesn't guarantee a well-paying job. You might be saddled with student loans and other debt after you graduate. You dedicate at least four years of your time, energy, youth, and intellect to a pursuit that is incredibly challenging and perhaps not immediately financially rewarding. So…is it worth it?

You're Investing in Future Earnings

While there can be some argument that the short-term financial benefits of graduating from college are minimal, the long-term benefits are definite and many. True, you may not get a high-paying job right after graduation. But you have several things in your favor: a degree that distinguishes you in the job market, the potential for better long-term earnings than your non-college-educated counterparts, and academic training that ideally will provide you with important job-related skills like critical thinking and analysis.

When you're surrounded by people working toward degrees and people—like your professors—with advanced degrees, it can be easy to forget how unique of an opportunity it is to earn a college degree in the first place. It takes a lot to make it through college, and not everyone has the opportunity, ability, and determination to make their college graduation a reality.

According to the 2012 United States Census Bureau's *Statistical Abstract of the United States*, only 19.4 percent of the total American population over the age of twenty-five had a bachelor's degree in 2010. People eighteen and older (with earnings) who had a bachelor's degree had mean earnings of $56,665; those with only a high school degree had mean earnings of $30,627. Add up those differences year after year, decade after decade, and the financial benefits of earning your degree become clear. Debbie Kaylor, Director of the Career Center at Boise State University, pointedly notes that, "You really need to look at what you want to be doing 5–7 years out of college." The amount you earn in the future will likely have made your college education worth it.

The question becomes, then, not if you can afford to go to college but if you can afford not to go. Yes, your education will likely cost you an arm and a leg. But—as long as you graduate—it is an investment well worth making. It is expensive. You do have to sacrifice. But the concern you have about your financial decision to attend college can be a motivating factor, not a stressful one.

If you still find yourself stressed about the high cost of your education, try to imagine what stressors you would face ten years from now if you didn't have a degree. What kinds of jobs would you be eligible for? How would you distinguish yourself from other job candidates while looking for work? Where would you live? How would you pay for the basics of your life, like food, housing, health care, and personal needs? In essence: Would the financial stressors of your life be bigger or smaller than the ones you are facing in college? Would the financial stressors of your life be bigger or smaller than the ones you would face if you did have a degree?

In essence, which would you financially regret and stress about more in the long term: graduating from college or dropping out?

There's More to Life Than Earning Money

In addition to improved career earnings, there are also the intangibles of how a college experience and a college degree can improve your life.

You go to college, after all, not necessarily to learn *what* to think but *how* to think.

Densil R.R. Porteous II, Director of Admissions at the Columbus College of Art & Design in Ohio, believes that college is a wise investment, both because of the employment potential and because of what college can do for your quality of life. "College teaches you how to socialize with people from different backgrounds. Learning is no longer just from a textbook as it was in high school, because in college your classmates and professors impart direct and indirect knowledge. There is a level of self-discovery that attending college guarantees and that isn't something drafted in a syllabus…it is something that is innate in the exploration of advanced learning and trying to understand why, or even if, it is important to you."

Solution #5: Handle Financial Emergencies

It's not uncommon to hear people joke about how college students don't live in "the real world." That's condescending and insulting—and also completely untrue. Just like others living in "the real world"—whatever that means—college students face unexpected financial situations and bona fide financial emergencies that can threaten to throw college plans off course.

You might be reliant on your car to commute to school and suddenly find yourself with an overwhelmingly large car-repair bill. A family member might have lost a job and not be able to help pay for your tuition and expenses. You might lose a scholarship. You might not be approved for loans. You might have a medical condition that, if not taken care of, will prevent you from returning to your classes. You might be facing an unexpected and significant tuition increase. No matter what your situation's specifics, however, the facts are undeniable: You are definitely facing a financial emergency. And with it comes a significant amount of stress.

While your current predicament may be unique to you, it's not uncommon for college students to face unexpected changes in their finances during their time in school. (Since, after all, students really do live in "the real world!") Because of this, there are resources you can go to if you find yourself facing a financial emergency.

Determine Exactly How Much You Need

First and foremost, try to get a general understanding of what kind of financial need you are looking at. How much will that car repair cost, for example, or how much will your uncle no longer be able to contribute toward tuition? Having a specific number in mind can give you a goal to focus on. Your stress will be better managed if you can say, "I need to find an additional $5,000" than if you say, "I can't afford to stay in school." After all, you very well might be able to stay in school— if you can find some money to fill in the unexpected financial gap.

Use Your School's Resources First

Once you know how much you need, make an appointment as soon as possible with your campus financial aid office. Do your best to keep your stress in check and your emotions under control. Of course, this is a stressful situation, and you should let the financial aid office know that. Have some specifics ready—like the exact amount of money you need to find, and by when—so that you can accurately communicate what your financial emergency is. Ask the financial aid staff member for his or her assistance and guidance. Can the financial aid office re-examine your financial aid package given these new circumstances? Are there any emergency funds available that can help you? Can your loan and/or scholarship amounts be increased? What other resources might the office be able to provide?

Then, talk to anyone on campus with whom you have a connection. Even if you don't think or aren't sure how they could help you financially, you owe it to yourself and to your education to at least make the effort. For example:

- Ask your professors if your department has any scholarships or other monies that you might now be eligible for.
- Ask your academic adviser what he or she has advised in the past for students in your situation—because, undoubtedly, there have been students in your situation.
- Ask the dean of students, your club adviser, and anyone else you see on a regular basis what they'd suggest or how they can help.

You'll never know what opportunities might arise unless you present yourself as someone looking for assistance.

Try to Make an Emergency Fund for the Future

Use a financial emergency as a reminder of how important it is to have some money put aside for the unexpected. Saving any money at all may seem incredibly difficult, if not impossible, but digging yourself out of an unexpected financial crisis might prove to be an even bigger obstacle. If you can work to set up a safety net for yourself, your stress levels caused by your delicate financial situation can decrease significantly.

If you find the idea of putting away some money in an emergency fund to be overwhelming, just think small. Try to save $5 a week—or even a month. Put your spare change into a jar and use that to start. Cut out small purchases, like coffee, once in a while and put the money into your emergency account. Even $25 or $50 can make a huge difference if, for example, your food money runs out a week before the semester ends or you don't have any money left for gas but still have one week left of commuting to class.

Use Your Network

You are your own best resource when it comes to facing a financial emergency. Tap into what you know, whom you know, what you're eligible for, and how hard you're willing to work to make things happen. A financial emergency can indeed be highly stressful—and it can also be a wonderful opportunity to learn more about all of the resources and people that are out there supporting you along your college journey.

Solution #6: Make Wise Financial Choices

One of the most wonderful aspects of being in college is the power you have to make your own choices. From where to live to what classes to take to which clubs to join to what events to attend, you are presented with innumerable choices all day, every day. Of course, some of those choices involve financial decisions. So how can you make sure that what you choose to do doesn't end up unintentionally sabotaging your financial situation?

What might at first seem like a fun, smart, or just an innocent decision can end up leading to an unexpected and large amount of financial stress. Consequently, knowing how to make wise financial choices is an important skill to learn. It will help reduce your stress, keep you in good financial health, and allow you to enjoy your time in school without constantly worrying about whether something was financially a good idea.

Stick to Your Budget

It can be very tempting to use money that should go toward college-related expenses for other purchases. But it's important to remember your budget and stick to it. A smart approach to take is to make a rule that you will ask yourself a set of questions whenever a situation meets a certain set of circumstances—when a purchase costs more than $10, for example, or when a choice involves spending money that previously hadn't been budgeted. Any time you find yourself in that situation, do a quick check-in with yourself by running through the following list of questions in your mind:

1. *Is this a want or a need?* Really, truly needing something is different from wanting something. Accordingly, needs should take a higher financial priority than wants.
2. *Have I done/experienced/purchased this before?* If so, do I really need to do so again? Some basic purchases need to be repeated. Others, perhaps, can be put on hold until after you graduate and have a steady income.
3. *Is this in my budget?* It can be nice and relaxing to go out to dinner if you know you can afford it. It can also be stress inducing and completely unenjoyable (at the time, or later) if you go when you know you shouldn't.
4. *Is there an alternative I can consider that will not cost as much?* Perhaps you really want to take a break and go out to eat; that's completely understandable. But perhaps you can make a smarter financial choice about doing so, such as going out to

lunch instead of dinner or going to a cheaper restaurant that still offers great food for a cheaper price.

5. *Will this short-term decision have a negative impact on my long-term financial picture?* It can be tempting to join others when they buy tickets for a concert, plan a weekend escape, or otherwise spend money in a way you know you shouldn't. Doing so, however, might wreak absolute havoc on your budget. Will the enjoyment of this short-term purchase be completely negated by the stress that follows? If so, back out while you can.

Listen to Your Gut

Even if you're managing your money for the first time, you likely have a general inkling about when you're making a smart financial choice and when you're not. And while having a budget and tracking your money can help inform your spending decisions, your gut can also be a factor to consider.

Do you know, if you listen to that feeling in your stomach, that the purchase you're about to make is a bad idea? If so, wise up and listen to your smart self. You can easily avoid unnecessary financial stress by making reasonable, informed choices that don't put you in a bind.

Solution #7: Work While You're in College

Some students work in college because they need to; others work in college because they want to. Regardless of your circumstances, working in college is bound to both alleviate and contribute to your stress.

Having a job while in school, of course, has many benefits. You'll earn some income, gain experience, build your network, and have additional human and financial resources at your disposal. Ideally, your job also understands and is supportive of the demands you face as a college student.

Finding a Job That Fits with Your College Life

When thinking about or actually looking for a college job, there are a couple of important factors to consider:

- How much money will you need to make?
- How many hours can you work without taking time away from your classes and homework obligations?
- How much must you make an hour to meet your financial obligations or desires?
- What kind of experience would you like to have?
- What kind of environment do you want to work in?
- What kinds of skills would you like to leave the job with?
- What kinds of people do you want to add to your network and meet through your job?

Debbie Kaylor, Director of the Career Center at Boise State University, encourages students to work while in college for the many benefits jobs can provide. "Getting a job in your field of study or an industry of interest would be ideal so you can build your professional network, but regardless of where you work, remember that any job provides you with the opportunity to gain valuable skills and experiences that will be transferrable to your career as you graduate," she advises.

Additionally, any work experience that you gain during your time in college can help you after you graduate. There's no harm in making the most of any and all jobs you take as a student. For example, working retail at a clothing store might provide a discount on your clothes.

Working as a host or server at a local restaurant might provide you with free dinners during your shifts. Perhaps your job as an administrative assistant at a local insurance firm can translate into a job later, when you have your degree.

Balancing Schoolwork and Your Job

In addition to providing professional skills and experience, your job will ideally help alleviate some financial pressure and allow you to reduce stress in other areas of your college life. If you're going to be working, you might as well get as much out of it as you can. A quiet job that lets you study during slow periods, for example, can reduce your financial stress while also helping you get things done on your academic to-do list. Or a job that keeps you physically busy can help you incorporate exercise and activity into your already-busy schedule.

It's particularly important to find a healthy balance between a college job and your academics, however, given that your amazing work experience might be for naught if you don't have the degree to go with it.

Dr. Laura W. Perna, Professor at the Graduate School of Education, University of Pennsylvania, has done extensive research on the topic. She has found that "Many students experience tremendous worry, as they try to manage the often competing demands of working, school, and family responsibilities. Time is finite; spending time working limits the amount of time for other activities including engaging deeply in their academic work."

Because of these competing demands and the need for students to still have the time and energy to dedicate to their classes, Perna recommends that, when possible, students limit the amount of hours they work each week. "Available research shows that students who work 10–15 hours per week have higher persistence rates than other students, suggesting that some amount of employment may be beneficial," she notes.

Make Smart Money Choices Even When Working

While getting a job—and a paycheck—can initially decrease stress about finances, you still need to make smart choices about spending. Having a paycheck every two weeks doesn't necessarily mean you have the freedom to immediately spend what you've just earned. Upcoming expenses, emergency savings, and your budget all need attention. It can be tempting, especially on payday, to make impulsive choices about fun ways to spend your money. Ultimately, though, your job should help alleviate your financial stress, not contribute to it. You don't want to put in all the effort of having a job just to end up where you were when you started: not having enough money to cover your basic expenses.

Dealing with Work Stress

While some students work to have a little extra spending money or a little more cushion in their budget, some students work because they have to. Even if you need the money a college job provides, you definitely don't need the extra stress. So what can you do if you're faced with both the need to work and the simultaneous and seemingly contradictory need to do well in school?

You have more options than you might think when it comes to employment opportunities. If you need to reduce the stress related to working while in college, think critically about what factors are in your control. Ask yourself these questions:

- **Can you change where you work?** If you have a long commute that is taking time away from your other obligations, see if you can work closer to home or closer to campus. Check to see if telecommuting is an option with the job you have or with an alternative. If you can't modify your current job's location, it might be time to see if you can find a new job that can fit the bill.

- **Can you change when you work?** If you find yourself having to work late and on weekends, see if there is a way you can move your schedule around. Perhaps working in the mornings, during lunch, or even in the early afternoon will help you be better able to deal with your other responsibilities. If you have a pretty difficult work schedule, see if you can swap your shift(s) with some coworkers, even if only occasionally. You might surprise yourself at the ways you creatively spend your time when you have an unexpected afternoon or evening off.

- **Can you change how you work?** If you are the type of person who likes to work hard at everything you do, you should be proud of your work ethic. That being said, it can sometimes become overwhelming to give your all to everything you're involved with in college. Since graduating is your ultimate goal, realize that it's perfectly fine to put in a good effort—in contrast to your *best* effort—with your college job. As long as you do what you need to, you can stress a little less about being the absolute best. Similarly, if you hold a managerial or supervisory position that is causing high levels of stress, see if you can reduce your responsibility level at work. Assuming that you can financially adjust, it can do wonders for your stress level if you can dedicate your energy to school and worry less about your work obligations.

A college job should complement your time in college, not detract from it. While some aspects of a college job can be stressful, they should be small, short-term stressors that come from a holiday rush or a busy day. Even if the financial benefits of your job are good, a job that collectively adds more stress to your life is one that likely needs adjusting—or replacing.

Solution #8: Save Money in Small and Simple Ways

College life is complicated, but it can be surprisingly simple to figure out how to save money in small ways. No matter how good you think you are at saving money, there are nearly always new and creative ways to explore.

Wants versus Needs

Perhaps the best way to reduce your spending is to start distinguishing between your wants and your needs. Wants are things you like to have around, things that make your college life easier or more enjoyable, things that you prefer in a particular way. Needs are things that you must have to function personally and academically.

For example, you *need* Internet access during your time in school for research, for participating in online discussions for class, and for submitting your assignments. In contrast, you *want* cable so you can watch sports or TV shows during your relaxation time. If you need to be spending less money, start looking closely at how much you're spending on your wants. Before making any purchase, large or small, pause for ten seconds and ask yourself: "Do I really need this or do I just want it? And if I do need this, is there another time or place I can get it that will cost less?" You might surprise yourself at how much you can reduce your spending—and your stress levels—by making this simple distinction.

You can also track how you're spending your money over a few days, as discussed in the budgeting section. Write down every penny and where it goes. Whereas you might usually just track how much you spend on food, start documenting what kind of food you buy and when and where you buy it. Then, after you have several days' worth of data, take a look at what kinds of things you can trim. Do you usually buy a coffee from the coffee shop in the afternoon? If so, could you replace it with something you brought from home? If you did that, how much money would you save? If you packed a snack each day instead of buying something on the quad, how much extra money would you have at the end of the week? What if you carpooled with a friend just one day a week to campus? What would you save on your commute by the end of the month?

Within your basic needs—food, housing, and school costs—you'll find wants that comprise them. For example, if you're going to rent an apartment, do you want your own place or do you need to have a roommate? Similarly, do you want to go out to eat a lot but need to learn to cook more to save money? Grabbing something at a campus café on your way to or from class might seem easy, but making your own sandwich in advance can be much less expensive.

Thinking creatively about your resources can also turn small choices into big savings. When there's a gap between your expenses and the money you have available, look to your own internal resources as a means of bridging that divide. You can change your spending habits, look at the details of your spending, and see what services you can provide to others, all of which can help increase your financial resources—and reduce your stress.

The seemingly simple and tiny choices you make on a daily basis all have consequences—big and small, financial and nonfinancial, stressful and nonstressful. Being mindful about each of those choices and whether or not they're being made with sound financial judgment can be a great way for you to save money, reduce at least a little bit of your financial stress, and emerge from college as someone who knows how to handle his or her money well.

Solution #9: Prepare for Life after College

All the loan papers you sign and all the hours of experience you gain in college have a direct impact on your life after school. The steps you take now as a student can prove to be of great financial benefit to you long after you've tossed your graduation cap.

Thinking of what your financial life will be like after you graduate can be both exciting and terrifying. Your imagined life of a great job, awesome apartment, and carefree social life can be punctured by the realities and stress of your financial situation. It's perfectly reasonable to be a little stressed when thinking about what your financial life after college will look like. But you don't want your stress about what might happen to sabotage your chances of what could happen. So what can you do as a student to make sure your financial choices empower your future instead of limit it?

Borrow Smartly

First and foremost: Be aware of all your debts. Ideally, you'd be able to pay for your college education on grants and scholarships, neither of which need to be repaid—but many students will need loans at one point or another.

If you're going to take out student loans, don't be stressed about them; choose, instead, to be smart about them. For example:

- Don't borrow more than you need.
- Shop around to make sure you're getting the lowest interest rate.
- Be aware of the conditions of any loans before you sign for them.

If something is stressing you out financially during your time in school, it likely will stress you out even more after you graduate. Do your best to make wise, informed choices about when, how, and from where you borrow money during your time in school.

Maximize Your College Experience for Increased Employability

Make yourself as marketable as possible while in college. True, you will graduate with a degree, which will help you as you look for work. However, you'll likely need more than just that slip of paper. Working while in school can help you gain experience and have references when you graduate.

As you explore your potential career interests, talk to your professors about any research or work opportunities they might know about. Work for the student newspaper, take a leadership role in your student club, and volunteer so that you can show a future employer that you have both book smarts and work smarts.

Don't be shy about using campus resources to make yourself more marketable. If you know you want to go into a certain field, head to the career center as soon as possible. (Conversely, the career center can also help you figure out what you might be interested in, even if you aren't sure yourself!) Talk to the counselors there about what your potential future employers are looking for. Think about getting a particular kind of job or internship, for example, so that you can have specific, high-demand skills before you graduate. Join (or start!)

a campus club that focuses on field-specific career options. Attend campus job placement and networking events and talk to as many recruiters as possible. After all, what do you have to lose—other than a shot at your dream job?

Spend Wisely on Yourself

During your time in college, your ultimate goal is to graduate. Along the way, of course, you are constantly working to improve yourself, to learn, to gain skills, and to grow in ways you might never have imagined. All of that energy deserves some investment along the way. Splurge and treat yourself to a nice, healthy breakfast before you interview for a job; skipping breakfast will leave you without energy and the mental sharpness you need to make a good impression. Be smart about buying nice but reasonably priced business attire so that, when you do interview—for everything from a summer internship to a full-time, postgraduate job—you can look professional.

Financial Stress: Conclusion and Highlights

You're in college because you're smart. Because of that, trust yourself to make smart choices about your money. If you have a budget, are tracking your expenses, and are being wise with your financial decisions, you can try to release any financial stress that may creep into your mind. You've got this!

- **Start with the basics of managing your money—and stick with them.** Make a budget, track your spending, and stick with your plan. Slow and steady care of your finances really can help keep your financial stress in check.

- **Keep things in perspective.** Yes, college costs a lot of money, but it will ultimately be worth it—financially and otherwise—when you graduate. Conversely, those short-term purchases that seem so tempting will not be worth it in the long run. Keep your focus on your goals and on what you need, not what you want.
- **Plan ahead.** If you're working during your time in school, make sure you're able to balance your work and academic schedules. Know in advance what resources are available to you in a financial emergency so that you can find solutions instead of feeling overwhelmed. Be courteous and timely (or early!) with the financial aid office so that your arrangements are always up-to-date and in order. Stress about finances is one thing that can be greatly reduced with a little planning.
- **Be mindful of how you spend your money.** Have a rule about when you need to pause, take a breath, and ask yourself a few important questions before making a big purchase. Think creatively about ways you can reduce your smaller purchases that end up resulting in big expenses by the end of the month. Understand where your money goes so that you can ensure what you have to spend goes toward what you need to spend it on. You don't want to end up stressing yourself out about not having enough money simply because you made poor choices that could have otherwise been avoided.
- **Understand that the choices you make now will have long-term effects on your financial life after college.** Debt that supports your education is an investment; debt that caters to your short-term desires can cause serious consequences—and stress. Treat your current and future self kindly by being smart about where, how, and when you make major financial decisions.

CHAPTER 3

Personal Stress

Even when it feels like college completely overtakes your life, in reality it's always only a part of your life. You still have all the things you had before—and that you'll have after—your time in school. Your friendships and other relationships may come and go and weaken and strengthen, but you'll always be connected to the people in your life in some way or another.

Sometimes, those personal connections can be helpful when it comes to managing your college stress. Other times, they can be downright harmful and exacerbate the stress you're already struggling with. And just like the other kinds of stress in your life, stress from your personal life can detract from your goals and your ability to graduate as planned.

Personal Stress: Identifying the Sources

While some relationships are nearly always stressful or stress-free, those are rare and easy to identify. Most personal relationships ebb and flow and change based on their context. Your best friend from high school, for example, may be great at helping you deal with a breakup but awful at giving financial advice; your mom, on the other hand, might be your best resource when it comes to handling your academic stress but a nightmare with her suggestions for dating.

As a college student, the relationships you have with your friends, your roommate(s), and your dating partners are usually relatively intense. After all, you likely spend the vast majority of your time focused on your college life in some way or another, meaning that your personal relationships within this context are heavily influenced by your college experience. If you're completely frustrated by your roommate's late-night shenanigans, it can be hard to focus in class; if you're going through a rough breakup, you might not be able to perform well on an upcoming exam.

When trying to identify the sources of your personal stress, then, it's important to try to look more at patterns than at specific instances. Do you have certain friends who are helpful most of the time? A cousin who's never much help? Thinking intentionally about the personal stress in your life requires you to take a step back; it is only through doing so that you'll truly be able to gain a wider perspective.

Personal Stress: The Five Questions

1. *Generally speaking, does my personal life add to or help me reduce the stress I face in college?* If you think, in general, about how you've felt over the past month, has your personal life added to or reduced the stress in your life? What about over the past six months? Past year? Past five years? Are there certain circumstances in your personal life that always seem to contribute to your personal stress? Are there certain people or circumstances that always seem to help reduce your personal stress?

2. *Which people in my life have a pattern of helping me deal with stress in a positive, healthy way?* If you are feeling seriously stressed-out, is there a family member whom you know you can call for support? Is there a friend who would move heaven and earth to give you a little TLC? Someone who knows

you're starting to stress out before you even do? Are there people who you think would be a positive, supportive influence if you reached out to them a little more? Do you have a romantic partner from whom you've learned a lot about managing stress? A long-term friend who always seems to cheer you up?

3. *Which people in my life have a pattern of adding stress in a negative way?* When you think of the three most stress-inducing people in your life, who comes to mind? What is your relationship like with them? Why do you categorize these individuals' presence as stressful? Are there people who have a pattern of introducing certain kinds of stress, or stress during certain periods of time, but who otherwise are beneficial to you? Do these people have anything in common? Do you have similar relationships with all of them? Or is their similarity only in that they all contribute stress to your personal life?

4. *Do I personally have a pattern of experiencing stress in certain relationships?* If you look back over the past six months, past year, and even past five years, can you see a pattern in certain kinds of relationships? For example, do you tend to have stressful and tumultuous romantic relationships? Do you tend to find social cliques that revolve around creating unnecessary stress? Or do you naturally gravitate toward personal relationships that help counterbalance the stress you feel in other areas of your life?

5. *What sources of stress do I have control over during my time in school?* What friendships might not be worth maintaining as you focus on college, given the stress they've added to your life up until this point? What romantic relationship(s) might be best for you to let go? What personal relationships should you

consider putting less effort into? Which ones can you work on improving? Which ones can you prioritize less as you shift your focus to your academics? Which relationships can you work on strengthening as you work to decrease your personal stress?

Finding Solutions

Once you've narrowed down the negative and positive influences on your personal life, you can more easily prioritize which need the most attention.

Solution #1: Follow the Golden Rule with Your Roommate

One of the areas students tend to stress about the most when preparing to start college is living with a roommate. Some students have never shared a room, some are nervous about sharing a room with someone they've never met, and some have simply never lived on their own before and aren't sure how to do so individually, much less with a bunch of strangers.

Living with a roommate, however, can be one of the highlights of your college experience. That doesn't mean it's not intimidating, though; it takes a brave soul to live in a (very) small space with someone you don't know (or with someone you barely know). It takes courage and a bold attitude about how you want to challenge yourself during your time in school. Use that attitude to focus on how you'll be a great roommate and have a positive experience instead of stressing over all the things that might (but probably won't) go wrong.

In essence, living with a roommate involves taking the basic standards of a positive, stress-free relationship and applying them to a new context. It can be helpful to approach your roommate relationship the same way you would a new friendship or other connection. In any new relationship, you probably wouldn't want to appear selfish or inconsiderate. And in order to avoid doing so, you simply have to begin with the essentials. When all else fails, following the golden rule—treating others as you would like to be treated—is a great place to start.

The basics of living with a roommate are just that: basics. They bear listing, though:

- Be kind. Say "hi" and "bye," make eye contact, and ask friendly questions.
- Be respectful. Ask before using someone else's things. Be clear about what you're willing to share and not share.
- Be mindful of how your actions might be affecting someone else's ability to study, sleep, or socialize.

Don't expect someone to be your best friend right away, if ever; he or she is your roommate first and foremost, and there's a difference. Similarly, being best friends with someone in high school (or even during your time in college) doesn't necessarily mean you'll be great roommates. The factors that make people great friends are different than those that make people great roommates. A friendship might naturally blossom—or it might not. Not becoming friends with your roommate doesn't necessarily mean that anyone is doing anything wrong. It just means that everyone is learning how to be roommates, which is really all that's required. Friendships are a different part of your college life; if they happen to form in your roommate situation, that's great. But it doesn't always happen, and expecting it to can add stress to your living situation.

It's Okay to Have Your Own Life

Even though they spend significant time together because of their housing situation, roommates often have very independent lives from each other. It can be helpful, and even healthy, to have a college life that has very little to do with your roommate. After all, if you shared everything together, things might get a little boring!

A roommate situation is a great opportunity to learn from and live with someone who is completely different from you. Work to establish your own individual life that your roommate relationship is a part of, not critical to. Your roommate will have ups and downs, just like you do. Check in and ask how things are going. Offer to help when and if you think it's needed. Take a step back when and if you think it's needed.

In essence: Be considerate. Even if things sometimes get stressful or you face the rare situation of needing to change roommates, you'll at least know you did your best. And with everything else you have to manage during your time in school, you won't have to stress about whether or not there's something you're doing wrong.

Proactive Skills and Tips for Living with a Roommate

Living with a roommate takes work; there's just no way around it. It's unrealistic to think that you'll meet a roommate, instantly hit it off, never have to talk about anything related to your roommate relationship, and live happily ever after.

Build a Strong Foundation

When you first are in touch with your roommate, you can work to keep stress out of your relationship by communicating well—and early. It's much less stressful to build a solid foundation for your roommate relationship from the beginning than it is to try to repair it later. Before you move in together, have at least one long conversation where you both go over your basic ideas and needs. You can plan as much as possible in advance of moving in together, while keeping in mind that you'll likely need to have a few conversations over the first week or two where you both check in about how things are going.

Forget all the images you've seen on TV and in movies about what life is like living in the residence halls or a college apartment. You don't need to live up to any expectation but your own. And since your biggest job while in school is to do well and graduate, focus more on what you need to make that happen—not on what you think you're supposed to be like. Not advocating for yourself is a recipe for disaster, not to mention major stress, as the year progresses.

While being proactive and talking with a roommate, you'll want to talk about:

1. What kinds of things you need in a living situation.
2. What kinds of expectations you'd like to set.
3. What you can do if problems start to arise.

The best way to have that conversation is to think about each of these topics in advance. Being proactive now can do wonders for preventing stress later.

- **Think about your ideal living situation.** What's it like when you first open the door? What does it look like? Sound like? Feel like? Who's there? What does your stuff look like? What does your roommate's stuff look like? What's it like in the middle of the day during the week? What's it like late at night during the week? What's it like in the middle of the day on the weekend? What's it like late at night during the weekend? What kind of living situation would you feel best in one week, one month, and six months from now?

- **Think about the expectations you'd like to set.** What do you expect from yourself as a roommate? What do you expect from your roommate? Is there a difference between the two? If so, what is that difference? Is it justified and fair? What do you think are reasonable expectations for roommates to have for each other? How much are you willing to step outside of your comfort zone? How much do you need to stay in your comfort zone?

- **Think about what you can do if problems start to arise.** How would you like your roommate to approach you if you're doing something that your roommate doesn't like? How do you feel most comfortable approaching your roommate if problems arise for you? How does your roommate want to be approached? When should something be considered a problem? What agreements can you make now about what to do if one person sees something as a problem but the other doesn't? What kinds of things are you not willing to compromise on later? What are the basics that you need in a living environment so that you can succeed in your classes? Asking yourself these questions before you talk to your roommate will help you realize what important messages about yourself and your preferences you should convey.

Consider an Agreement

It's also a smart idea to use a roommate agreement or similar document offered by your institution (or even found online) as a conversation starter. These agreements present an opportunity for you and your roommate to discuss basic rules about sharing space, sharing stuff, and your preferences around everything from having people over to how messy (or not) you like your room. While bringing up the topic may seem awkward at first, roommate agreements are pretty normal in college. Because everyone is new and living with someone they don't know at all (or at least don't know very well), agreements are more of a tool to facilitate a conversation than some kind of formal accountability document. Use a roommate agreement as part of your discussion about your and your roommate's preferences instead of as the main focus of the conversation. In essence, the agreement can guide the conversation and help clarify things. What you might think of as awkward usually ends up being pretty helpful; the agreement can help you clarify preferences and talk about topics you might not have thought of on your own.

It's much easier to talk about things when you're just starting out than it is when there's a conflict. Ideally, too, a roommate agreement can help prevent conflicts, since you'll both end up establishing some ground rules that can make sure everyone's needs are met and problems are avoided whenever possible.

Be Honest

No matter when or how you talk to your roommate, however, it's important to adequately and accurately reflect your lifestyle and your preferences. If, for example, you have grand plans to always keep your room clean and wake up early while in college, but you've always been really messy and love sleeping late, it's better to just be honest about what you're usually like. If you do end up totally changing your habits, you can address that change later. But for right now, look at your past patterns and what kinds of things help you best thrive and learn.

Additionally, don't be shy about advocating for what you need, even if you think it's silly or are worried about feeling embarrassed. If you need your room to be relatively quiet and neat so you can study, then say so. If you like to go to bed early, don't want alcohol in your room, don't want to share your food and clothes, don't want visitors over, and don't like loud music, that's perfectly okay, too. What's not okay is pretending like these things don't matter and then having a conflict later that could have otherwise been avoided.

Reactive Skills and Tips for Living with a Roommate

No matter how much you plan, however, there are undoubtedly going to be a few awkward situations and moments that happen with your roommate. Are those situations and moments going to be horrible? Probably not. But they will likely need addressing so that small conflicts don't turn into big, ugly stressful situations later.

Keep Calm

First and foremost, try not to talk to your roommate when your emotions are running high. Even if you walk into a situation—say, a loud party in your room the night before an important final—take a few moments to take a walk, get some perspective, and calm down. You want to have a productive conversation, after all, not a shouting match. When encountering a situation you want to address directly, take a deep breath and start with the basics.

Address the Facts

Think about what frustrates you the most in the conflict. Is it something your roommate is doing? Something your roommate is not doing? A pattern? One particular incident? How are you feeling as a result of what happened (or what's continuing to happen)?

Do your best to talk about the issue and the consequences it has for you. For example, you can note that when your roommate frequently eats all your breakfast food, you're stuck going to ROTC training on an empty stomach. You might be frustrated with the lack of respect you feel, the damage that your roommate's munchies are doing to your budget, or the simple fact that you're tired of being hungry. Knowing what frustrates you the most can help you—and your roommate— figure out what really needs to be addressed.

Propose a Solution

Lastly, think about what kind of solution you'd like to see. You may want to continue to vent about your roommate's annoying behavior, but if you don't have a goal for the conversation, your roommate may end up feeling attacked. Focus on how you can remedy the situation instead of dwelling on why it's a problem. That way, you both can feel like you are doing something to resolve the conflict—and any stress that has arisen because of it.

Solution #2: Practice Effective Roommate Communication

Perhaps the most important feature of any good roommate relation- ship is good communication. If you can't talk to your roommate about certain things, your stress level is undoubtedly going to increase as the semester progresses. "If roommates have open communication and are not scared to ask questions and engage one another, they can resolve potential conflicts before they ever start," observes Dr. Rameen Talesh, Dean of Students at the University of California, Irvine.

Good communication skills, however, are difficult to establish and maintain. There are seemingly endless factors influencing your college roommate relationship: academic obligations, cocurricular involvement, work, your social life, and an overall lack of time. While your to-do list may seem overwhelming more often than not, it's still important to keep communicating with your roommate. If you don't, you'll unfortunately find yourself with a major stressor in your life that could otherwise have been avoided.

So what does good roommate communication look like? Just like any relationship, there are some basics that are important to keep in mind.

Nip Problems in the Bud
Don't wait until things have become an enormous problem for one or both of you before addressing it. Deal with problems as they present themselves, as uncomfortable as that may be, or—better yet—be as proactive as you can about preventing problems in the first place.

"Don't let things build up, make sure to communicate, and be willing to compromise," recommends Talesh. He describes a common situation he encounters between roommates:

> *"I cannot tell you how many times a roommate will build up so much frustration and finally burst out with anxiety (to a roommate, friend, or family member). When the roommate finds out the information, they simply were unaware their behavior was having such a negative impact and are (and were) willing to change their behavior from the beginning...if they only knew about it. This is difficult because sometimes students share they were willing to hold in their frustrations because they did not want to 'hurt their roommate's feelings.' In the end, they create more stress for themselves when the issue could have been resolved*

if they would have shared their concerns openly. Being able to share information in a non- threatening or judgmental way goes a long way toward building a respectful roommate relationship."

Stick to Face-to-Face Roommate Talks

The way you communicate with your roommate matters a great deal as well. Lesley Levy, Assistant Dean of Student Affairs at Bowdoin College in Maine, has some essential advice for roommates. "My number one rule regarding roommate communication is: Don't say something in the social media world that you wouldn't say face-to-face to your roommate," she recommends. "Another proactive measure is engaging in verbal communication as opposed to notes or texts," Talesh also says. "Tone is something that cannot be interpreted with text messages and notes." That means speaking with your roommate—in person.

As you work to build a pattern of strong communication with your roommate, make it easier on everyone—including yourself—to talk directly, respectfully, and honestly with each other. If you're going to make the effort to communicate well, you don't want to sabotage your efforts (and increase your stress) by going about it in a way that could easily be misinterpreted.

Truly Listen

Good communication skills include good listening skills, too. When talking to a roommate, try to listen as much as (if not more than) you talk. There could be a legitimate reason why your roommate is suddenly acting so funky. You might hear a side of the story you hadn't considered, or you might realize that you both are right about an issue and need to work to find some middle ground.

Focus on the Real Problem

While listening is important, it's also wise to think carefully not just about what you're saying but how you're saying it. When talking with your roommate, try not to make things personal. Keep the focus on behaviors and actions, not personalities. If you don't like that your roommate's boyfriend is over all the time, for example, try to discuss setting some limitations on having visitors and how having people over too frequently prevents you from studying or sleeping. That way, your roommate won't be defensive about his or her boyfriend as a person, and the conversation can focus more on the problem instead of the people behind it.

Similarly, telling your roommate, "You are SO LOUD!" is much less productive than "I want to talk about when we should be keeping the room quieter." The latter focuses on the problem and the solution; the former focuses on the person. If you thought your situation was stressful now, wait until things inadvertently get personal. Aim to reduce the stress of your conflict, not exacerbate it.

Ask for Professional Help If You Need It

If you are feeling like you don't know where to start when communicating with your roommate, like you're trying your best but nothing is working, or like your roommate is being stubborn and not listening to what you have to say, you can always reach out for a little advice or intervention.

Professional staff members and student workers are specifically trained to provide advice, give neutral feedback, and even intervene if necessary in roommate conflicts. If you can't communicate with your roommate directly, try connecting with someone who can help. Doing so, after all, is a way of communicating, too—and a way to ideally reduce the stress for everyone involved in the situation. You can talk to a resident adviser (RA), a professional staff person in your residence hall or apartment building (such as a hall director or area coordinator), or someone in the residence life or dean of students office. Everyone in these positions and offices is trained to help students with roommate situations. They can be a great resource if you need a little advice or even someone to help calm down and mediate your conflict.

Solution #3: Turn Conflicts Into Solutions, Not Stressors

When a conflict arises between you and your roommate, you have a few options available to you:

1. You can ignore the problem, hoping it goes away...which won't happen.
2. You can address the problem but not the behavior behind it, which often means the problem (i.e., the behavior) will present itself again at a later date.
3. You can turn the conflict into a solution instead of a reoccurring, stress-inducing pain in the brain.

While a proactive approach, smart reactive skills, and strong communication all play an important role in resolving roommate conflicts, it's also wise to focus not only on finding a solution but also on the long-term feasibility of that solution. You have enough to deal with without having to repeatedly address a roommate issue that has bothered you since the first week of classes.

The First Offense

If something is bothering you for the first time, be honest with yourself about what's at the heart of the issue. Do you feel judged? Disrespected? Annoyed? Ignored? Could it be that stress from other areas of your college life is seeping over into this area, and you're overreacting? What advice would you give to a friend in a similar situation? If you could wave a magic wand and resolve the conflict, what would the solution look like? Is that solution reasonable? If not, how can you find a compromise? If so, how can you get there?

Additionally, Ray P.R. Quirolgico, EdD, Assistant Vice President for Student Development at Saint Louis University in Missouri, encourages students to consider what role they themselves might be playing in the situation. "The first thing to do if you experience a conflict with someone (like your roommate)," he recommends, "is to ask yourself: What am I contributing to this conflict? Remember that all relationships (friendships, relationships with family members, dating partnerships, and even roommates) involve more than one person."

Repetitive Behaviors

If a repeated behavior is bothering you, try to look more deeply into the root of what's stressing you out about it. Have you addressed the problem before but felt unsatisfied with the solution? Is your roommate ignoring or not following through with your requests for change? Are you being unreasonable? Is your roommate being unreasonable? What are the three biggest factors that you think might be causing this issue to reappear?

Many roommates, for example, disagree about cleanliness and sleep schedules. If you and your roommate(s) are not on the same page in those areas, rest assured that you're not alone in dealing with them—and that some general ground rules will help in preventing further conflict down the road.

Maintain Perspective

When a roommate conflict appears, it's not necessarily because anyone is doing anything wrong. It's simply a normal course of events for any two (or more) people living together. How you handle that conflict, however, can have a significant impact on the rest of your college life—and your stress levels. Finding short-term, unsatisfying, unreasonable, or unworkable solutions to roommate conflicts only perpetuates those conflicts and causes the stress for everyone involved to slowly grow. Address what you can, when you can, with the resources you have available to you so that you can transform conflicts into a sustainable, satisfying living situation that helps reduce your stress instead of contribute to it.

Solution #4: Make the Most of College Friendships

When you first arrive in school, the best way to meet friends is to take a deep breath, get out of your room, and talk to as many people as possible. This can be challenging if you're shy or introverted, but it's incredibly important. One thing to keep in mind is that, most likely, everyone in your class is new. Very few, if any, students have friendships that they don't want to share or expand on. Many students only know one or two other people on campus—if that—so meeting people is something you're all doing together, even if you feel alone.

Where to Meet New People

Most college campuses support a friendly environment. Try not to let shyness or fear of the unknown make you feel stressed or uncomfortable. If anything, the unique culture of college removes the usual stressors of making friends and introducing yourself to people. Since everyone is new in all kinds of environments (new to college, new to the residence hall, new class starting, new to a club), it's completely normal—if not expected—that you'll strike up conversations and friendships with people on a continual basis. Even seniors will likely meet new people and form new friendships during their final few months in school.

If you're feeling stressed about where to meet people and how to make more friends, rest assured that there are all kinds of ways to go about it—and that they can be fun. If you're looking for ways to reach out, think about:

- Joining a club.
- Working for the newspaper.
- Getting a campus job.
- Joining or starting a study group.
- Joining or starting an intramural sports team.
- Volunteering on or off campus.
- Joining a fraternity or sorority.
- Seeing what leadership positions are available in your residence hall or other living community.
- Joining a ride-share program if you commute to campus.
- Going to as many campus events as possible and talking to people.

And if all else fails, try to talk to one new person a day. Something will stick!

Be Yourself

Ray P.R. Quirolgico, EdD, Assistant Vice President for Student Development at Saint Louis University in Missouri, says to stay true to yourself as you seek out new college friendships. "If you are not a big party animal, then choose to abstain from that scene and hang out with other people making choices similar to you. If you feel an affiliation for a certain political party, don't feel compelled to attend the meetings of the other political party clubs just to look cool," he advises. "But by all means, seek out people different from you and find out what you can learn from them and try to imagine what lessons different people have to offer to you. Often, the differences you encounter help you clarify and confirm the person you are." The key is not to compromise your own ideals and preferences to try to fit in with a certain crowd.

Be Patient

You shouldn't expect solid, positive, healthy friendships to appear immediately. You might feel a lot of pressure to form very fulfilling, lifelong friendships in college—you may have seen them idealized on TV or in the movies; you may have heard your parents or other family members talking about great college friends whom they've stayed close with for many years.

Because college can be such a life-changing experience—and one that you share with the same people for several years—forming long-term friendships is definitely a benefit of your time in school. Anticipating that those friendships are to be expected and will happen without effort, however, can put unrealistic expectations on you and on your potential friends. The friendships will come—just be patient.

College Friendships Can Come and Go

Friendships in college take on a different form and context than other friendships in your life. You and your college friends are all living a shared experience, and through that can come some incredible bonding. But college is also a very growth-intensive experience that may cause you to change and develop in ways you weren't expecting. Because of that, you might find that you make some friends early on who aren't going to be lifelong friends. On the other hand, you might find that you're immediately very close to your college friends. That's all okay. Growing in and out of friendships means you're doing everything right, not doing something to stress out about.

Make Sure Your Friends Support Your Goals

It's important to have positive, healthy friendships in college. There are a lot of things to distract you from the stress of your studies, which is great—but you need to be sure you have your eye on your main goal: to graduate. If you find that your college friends are taking away from your academic performance, are not supportive of you when you say you need time to study, or otherwise are adding stress and negativity to your college experience, it's okay—if not downright mandatory—to find some new friends. One of the benefits of becoming more independent and managing your own college life is that you have both the choice and the power to be friends with whomever you please. Friendships should accentuate your success in school, not detract from it. If your friendships are stressing you out, it's time to look elsewhere.

On the flip side, however, strong, supportive friendships can turn into your family of sorts during your time in school.

○ **Straight from a Student: Supportive Friends**

Sriya Bhumi, a junior at Union College in New York, definitely relies on her friends as a family-like support system. "I talk to my friends about any stresses in my life," she says. Friends you meet in college can be a great alternative for helping you process through and come up with solutions for your stress. Because college friends can directly relate to and understand the stressors of your college life, they can be a great resource in ways that your other support systems cannot. From academics to personal issues, college friends can help you find solutions to the things causing the most angst during your time in college. "Don't keep your stress bottled up," Bhumi suggests. "Talking things out also allows you to make sense of a situation. People's advice helps you cope with stress. When family isn't something that's readily available, your friends are the next best things. They soon will seem like a part of your family."

Solution #5: Maintain High School Friendships in a Healthy Way

It can be difficult to maintain your high school friendships while you're in college. You might run into a variety of challenges with them:

- You might be in college while your friends back home are not.
- Everyone from your high school group might have gone to college in different places.
- You might all have gone to the same school but be involved in totally different things.

It's important to realize that your high school friendships will undoubtedly change significantly during your time in college. Though that can be stressful, it's something that naturally happens as people grow and change and move off in different directions. Some high school friendships will be strengthened by college, whereas others might abruptly end or gradually fade away. It's up to you to think about which friendships you want to maintain, which friendships you want to let slip away, and which ones you just want to let be.

When You "Outgrow" Your High School Friends

Similar to your college friendships, your high school friendships should add to and support your efforts in college. If your old friends are mocking you for how much you study, how you choose to spend your time, or the choices you make as a college student, it might be time to realize that your high school friends are just that: high school friends. Your time in college might require different support systems and people.

That shift, however, doesn't necessarily mean anyone has done anything wrong or that you're passing judgment on anyone. It just means that the friends and friendships that worked in high school may no longer work in college. If and when your high school friends fade away, it's okay to let any stress you're feeling over that loss fade away, too.

When High School Friends Are a Fun Connection to Your Past

In contrast, however, you might also notice that your high school friendships are a great way to keep you grounded and connected to your life before college. It can be fun to catch up with old friends back home and hear the latest about how everyone is doing. It can also be great to have people who knew and loved you before, during, and even after college.

"Because so much of the college experience will challenge and change you, it's always nice to have perspective that grounds you and helps keep you steady as you learn and grow," says Ray P.R. Quirolgico, EhD, Assistant Vice President for Student Development at Saint Louis University in Missouri. "I think that's what existing friendships can be: they are a connection to your past."

If this is the case, celebrate accordingly. Having friendships that can survive the test of time is a gift. Enjoy the connections you have with these friends and use them to help keep you—and your college stress levels—in check.

Solution #6: Stress-Free Dating

Dating in college is like no other setting. Some people are in long-term, healthy relationships; some are in long-term, drama-filled relationships. Some date here and there; some love the hook-up scene. Some people think they're hooking up when they're really in a relationship (with the same hook-up) even though they don't want to call it a relationship... but everyone knows it really is. Some people are perfectly happy being single. And, of course, some people fall in multiple categories, sometimes all at the same time.

Just like dating before and after college, dating while you're in college can be great. You can pretty much make whatever choices you'd like, and, as long as you're making smart choices, you can live your life without too much stress.

When Dating Becomes Stressful

Sometimes, however, your dating choices and behaviors might turn into major sources of stress. Perhaps the approaches you thought would help you relieve stress actually add to it. Or perhaps the aspects of being (or not being) in a relationship that you thought would be stressful have turned out to be completely the opposite.

Fortunately, dating in college is something you have complete control over. Unlike your classes, you don't have to take prerequisites or carry a certain course load. If you want to date, fine. If not, also fine. If you want to try to date, want to simply (and responsibly) enjoy the hook-up scene, want to take a break, or want to not even think about it, you can do as you please.

Safety First

One important thing to note about dating: Be responsible. If you want to live your life and be treated like an independent adult, you need to make choices like one. That means talking about sexual history and using protection. No, it may not be fun to bring up with a partner, but yes, you still have to do it. One instant way to add stress—and lots of it—to your personal life is to have to deal with an unexpected STD, STI, pregnancy, or other sexual health issue. Be smart! Some students are more likely to make poor choices in the first few weeks of school as they adjust to the college scene— be especially cautious then, as poor decisions during even the first week of class can have a major impact on the rest of your time in school (if not your entire lifetime).

Take Note of What Makes You Feel Less Stressed

The college dating scene is what you make of it. The key element to focus on, however, is not necessarily what you are doing, but how you feel after it. If you go on a few quiet dates and feel relaxed afterward, that type of dating might work well for you. If one-on-one dinners make you feel nervous and stressed, they might not be the right choice for this point in your life. Maybe hanging out in groups is less stressful for you. If your behavior, choices, or relationships are adding stress to your college life, you have complete control to change them.

It can be fun and a great learning experience to step outside of your comfort zone and engage in the college dating scene in new and unexpected ways. You might find yourself surprised at the kinds of people you're attracted to, for example. As long as you're being safe and respectful with your partner(s), trying new and unexpected things in your dating life can be a great experience. That exploration, after all, can help you figure out what kinds of romantic partners you enjoy—and don't enjoy. Ideally, your intimate relationships and experience with the college dating scene will help you learn more about yourself, provide companionship, connect you with amazing people, and ultimately complement your college experience—not add stress to it.

Solution #7: Learn to Handle Relationship Problems

Even the best romantic relationships can be strained by the stresses of college. Homework, finances, time management, cocurricular obligations—if something is part of your college life, it's part of any dating relationship you have, too.

You may have thought that your high school relationship could survive the transition. You may have thought that your new relationship was going to be a positive aspect of the academic year. Or you may have thought that being in a long-distance relationship was going to be easier than it really is. So just what can you do if you find that you're dealing with relationship problems—and the stress that comes with them—during your time in college?

A relationship can be a great way to learn and grow in this regard, but that learning and growth should be a positive, productive, healthy experience. If you find that your relationship is not empowering that process, look at how that can be changed.

How you handle relationship stress depends on a variety of factors. The relationship context, the length of the relationship, your other obligations, and your dedication to the relationship all play important roles in whether or not you can transform stress into enjoyment. After all, your romantic partner should be a positive, healthy influence in your life, not something that complicates your time in school. When thinking about your relationship(s), consider the following questions.

Where Are Each of You?

What's the context of your relationship? Is one of you in college and the other not? Is one of you studying abroad while the other is still on campus? Are you both in college but at different schools? Are you on the same campus and seeing each other a little *too* often? (Believe it or not, that can put a strain on a relationship.) If you rarely get to see each other, however, you might face a different kind of stress.

Think about the context of your relationship and how it might be adding stress (or not). Specifically, ask yourself:

- Do you need to see your partner more? Less? How much of that is in your control?
- What are your personal interactions like? Are you satisfied with them?
- What are your electronic interactions like? Are you satisfied with them?
- When you think of seeing this person unexpectedly, how does that make you feel?

If you find that your interactions are stressing you out, you might want to consider your involvement in the relationship. And if you find that you want to see your partner more, it can be helpful to focus your energy on making that happen or, if you can't see each other more frequently, on making the most of how you can still communicate and connect.

Long-Distance Relationships

Long-distance relationships in particular can be challenging during college. That's not to say that you shouldn't try, of course—just that you should be aware of what role your long-distance relationship will play in your college life and what it will require.

One thing you can do to increase a long-distance relationship's chance for success is to communicate early with your partner. "Before leaving for college, have open and honest conversations with your relationship partner about what you each expect in your separate and in your combined futures," suggests Ray P.R. Quirolgico, EdD, Assistant Vice President for Student Development at Saint Louis University in Missouri. He recommends talking about the following questions with your partner before you leave for college:

- Are we allowed to date other people?
- How often should we expect to communicate? Should it be via phone call? Text? Video chat?
- When will we see each other?
- How should we bring it up if something's not working?

Having answers to these questions before you arrive on campus can help eliminate any stress that might result from making decisions based on relationship assumptions instead of agreements.

Being close—both physically and emotionally—in any relationship is usually, of course, a good thing. When that's not possible, however, the effects can sometimes be stress inducing. Try to take a step back and analyze, at a time when you're calm, how your physical location has an impact on your relationship.

How Long Have You Been Together?

What's the length of your relationship? Sometimes, people feel committed to a relationship simply because they've been involved together for a long time. Is that happening in your situation? Do you feel more invested in your relationship because you've been together for so long? Or, conversely, have you just started a relationship and are surprised at how much intensity it's brought into your life already?

While the length of your relationship shouldn't be the only factor in helping you determine how to handle stress within the relationship, it is an important thing to consider. Are you feeling so stressed because you've invested so much? Or is the amount of stress you're experiencing unreasonable given how short a time you've been together? The time you've spent with the other person can help you gauge whether the relationship itself is causing stress or whether you're just going through a stressful period. Additionally, what you invested thus far can help you better gauge whether you'd like to continue with that level of investment or if, for your own health and stress levels, it's time to move on.

Are You Being Pulled in Too Many Directions?

What other obligations might be causing stress in your relationship? Are you too heavily involved cocurricularly to give the time and energy you want to this relationship? Is your course load larger than usual, more involved than usual, or simply one that requires a lot of your mental focus right now? Are there other stressors, like your finances or family, that are taking up a lot of your free time?

The most important thing to do is prioritize when trying to figure out what external obligations are possibly putting stress on your relationship. There are some priorities that are not very flexible during your time in college—for example, doing well in your classes, meeting your financial obligations, and taking care of your physical self. If your partner or relationship is requiring you to compromise basics like these, then it's no wonder you're so stressed-out.

A partner who wants you to rearrange your most important priorities is asking too much of you, particularly when you're working so hard to better yourself and your life with a college degree. Keep your focus on what matters most. Sometimes, you might be able to reorganize your other commitments so that they don't add so much stress to your relationship; other times, you might need to acknowledge that your relationship is the main cause of stress and, consequently, needs to be significantly adjusted or let go.

Personal Stress: Conclusion and Highlights

While the personal relationships you make, grow, and maintain during your time in school can be life changing, they can also be challenging. Most relationships will ebb and flow as you grow as a person. This can be difficult to accept, but it's important to make sure the personal relationships you have during your time in school help support your success instead of detracting from—and adding stress to—your efforts.

- **Living with a roommate can be a great experience.** With a little work, some realistic expectations, and a considerate attitude, living with a roommate can be one of the highlights of your college years.

Approach having a roommate as something to celebrate and enjoy, instead of something to worry about and stress over.

- **Honest communication is a critical element of a successful roommate relationship.** Talk with your roommate before living together—and thus in advance of any problems developing—about your expectations and needs. Spend some time building a strong foundation so that, as you navigate through the other stressful aspects of your college life, your roommate relationship doesn't make things worse.

- **Friendships will take on an entirely new form and meaning during your time in school.** It's completely normal for the friends and friendships you made before going to college—particularly in high school—to fit into your life in a different way. These changes can be positive, negative, or a little of both. Focus on eliminating the friendships that add stress to your life and investing in the friendships that support you.

- **College friendships will also take on new forms.** Friendships in college will likely be different than those you've developed during other periods in your life. Be patient with yourself as you meet new people and form friendships while you adjust to college. If you find yourself struggling to form solid friendships, focus on taking the smaller steps first, like becoming more involved in your college community or talking to at least one new person every day.

- **While dating in college can be complicated, your approach to it can be very simple.** Whether you want to (responsibly) hook up, be in a long-term relationship, or not even think about dating, as long as you're doing what feels right for you (and being safe), you're making the right choice. If your involvement or lack of involvement in the college dating scene is causing you stress, then think seriously about adjusting your behavior, choices, and expectations. Unlike your academics or financial aid, for example, you have complete control over this area of your college life. If something is stressing you out, change it.

- **Romantic relationships will probably need to adjust during your time in school.** Whether you're in a long-distance relationship or dating someone across the hall, it's important to keep things positive. Ideally, your romantic partner will support you and your goals. If you find that your partner and your relationship with him or her is adding stress to your life or otherwise taking your focus off of your other priorities, it's time to reconsider your relationship. After all, you're working your tail off to do well during your time in school and to graduate with your degree in hand. Any and all of your romantic relationships should be supportive of that journey instead of adding stress along the way.

CHAPTER 4

Physical Stress

While you may not have realized that college is a physically challenging time in your life, it is! Think about it: You wake up in an uncomfortable bed—probably tired—and walk or bike to class. You sit for a while, possibly go to another class, then get something—probably not super healthy—to eat. Then you're off to more class, possibly a nap, homework, cocurricular meetings, and social activities.

This kind of routine can take your body from one extreme to another: rushing to class, then being motionless. Not eating breakfast, then eating unhealthily at lunch and dinner, and eating at infrequent and irregular times. (Greasy pizza at 2:00 A.M., anyone?) You might drink too much caffeine or too many energy drinks in your attempts to stay awake, which end up also causing you to not rest fully when you finally do head to bed. You may feel that you don't have the time to exercise regularly, and when you do get to sleep at the end of the day, you probably aren't able to stay asleep for as long as you'd like.

Other, longer-term routines also can have stress-inducing consequences. Your alcohol use on the weekends might be leading to poor decision-making; your constant rushing around hasn't allowed your body to really rest when it needs to. Your immune system might not be at its best and your lack of regular exercise is catching up with you.

Your physical health is a major factor in your success. If you're constantly sleep deprived, low on energy, not eating well, and fighting off one sickness after another, succeeding in college will become exponentially more difficult. And with everything else you have to manage, dealing with a body that won't cooperate is not something you want to add to the equation.

Physical Stress: Identifying the Sources

Identifying what's causing your physical stress is often easier than trying to identify other sources—like the personal ones—of your college stress. After all, there's a pretty direct cause-and-effect relationship between the physical sources of your stress and their consequences. If you're tired, you probably need more sleep, for example. So what kinds of things should you consider as you try to break down the basics of your college-based physical stress?

Physical Stress: The Five Questions

1. *When do I physically feel the best?* What times of day do you have the most energy? When do you feel like you can physically do anything? What kinds of foods does your body respond to most positively? What kinds of exercise do you like? What kinds of physical things do you most look forward to doing? What do you and your body love about doing them? How do you know when your body is feeling really great? What kinds of things can you accomplish when you're physically being kind to your body? How do you know that a new physical choice is good for you? What kinds of signs does your body give you when it's physically healthy?

2. *When do I physically feel the worst?* When does your body really
   struggle to perform basic daily tasks? What times of day are
   hardest for you to make yourself rally? What do you most
   dread doing physically? Why is this so challenging for you and
   your body? When are you the most physically uncomfortable?
   What kinds of physical tasks do you try to avoid? Why? How
   do you know that a new physical choice is adding stress to
   your body instead of helping it? What kinds of signs does your
   body give you when it's physically unhealthy?

3. *What do I need to be physically healthy?* How much sleep do
   you personally need to feel rested and to function well? How
   much—and how often—do you need to eat? What kinds of
   foods do you need to eat regularly? What kinds of foods do
   you need to avoid? How much exercise do you need to get?
   How frequently do you need to exercise? What kinds of exercise does your body seem to thrive on? What kinds of foods,
   activities, or habits help you physically feel your best? What
   kinds of foods, activities, or habits help you mentally feel the
   best about your physical self?

4. *What have my short-term patterns and their consequences been?*
   What has your physical stress been like over the past week?
   Two weeks? Month? How have you been treating yourself
   physically? How have you been meeting your basic, individual
   physical needs? What kinds of things have influenced whether
   or not you were able to meet your basic, individual physical
   needs? How has meeting those needs—or not meeting those
   needs—made you physically feel? What kinds of activities or
   habits have worked well for you physically? What kinds of
   activities or habits have not worked well for you physically?

What have been the three main sources of physical stress? What have been their consequences?

5. *What have my long-term patterns and their consequences been?* What has your physical stress been like over the past six months? Year? Two years? How has your physical self changed over those time periods? Has it changed for the better? For the worse? What have been the biggest factors influencing your physical health—positively and negatively—over the long-term? How much control do you have over those factors during your time in college? What long-term physical patterns would you like to change? What long-term physical patterns would you like to maintain? What kind of relationship have you had with your physical self over the past few years? Have you treated you body kindly? Has your body treated you kindly? What level of physical stress, on a scale of one to ten, do you think your body has endured over the past six months? Year? Two years? How will that increase, decrease, or stay the same during your time in school?

Finding Solutions

Fortunately, knowing where your physical stressors are coming from and how your body physically manifests stress can help you decide where best to focus your efforts on improving your physical self. Even a few small, simple acts of physical self-care can really affect your ability to function well and manage your stress.

Solution #1: Exercise

You might think that you don't have time to exercise while in college. You're wrong.

It's easy to forget about exercise—and other basic forms of physical self-care—during your time in school. If you have a difficult time (like most students do) fitting in all your academic work amidst everything else, something has to give. If you have to choose between studying for an hour for your upcoming midterm or running on the treadmill, a good student would obviously choose the study time…right?

Not necessarily. As you've no doubt heard throughout your life, exercise can help you in all kinds of ways:

- It gives you more energy and more focus.
- It helps you feel better physically and function more efficiently.
- It's an essential part of maintaining an overall healthy lifestyle.

Given that all of these benefits help you perform better academically, why would you ever let exercise fall by the wayside?

Yes, finding the time to exercise can be a challenge. You already have to be quite selective about when, where, and how you spend your time. When priorities get out of balance, stress can build up and make things worse. Yet making the time for regular exercise can help you maintain the equilibrium you'll need for a healthy, stress-free college experience.

Trying to get more, or at least regular, exercise during your time in college can feel like one more thing to do when you're already overburdened. The best part of frequent exercise, however, is that it nearly always proves beneficial. It can be social, fun, and healthy. And it can be a lot easier to incorporate into your schedule than you might think.

Fitting Exercise Into Your Schedule

Perhaps the best way to incorporate exercise into your daily life is to think creatively about it. You're probably a great multitasker, so put those skills to work. Some creative ways to add exercise to your schedule can include:

- If you're involved in a leadership role and have to meet regularly with other leaders, see if you can do so during a weekly run or brisk walk. You can talk, get a great workout in, do some planning, and spend some time outside together.
- If you need to spend a certain amount of hours listening to a foreign language for a class, do so while exercising in the gym.
- If you need to get reading done, watch a film, or even just think about a thesis for your midterm, dedicate yourself to doing so while on a treadmill. (If you have to, reserve the equipment in advance so that the thirty minutes you allocated in your calendar for working out can happen as scheduled.)
- If you need to study for an upcoming midterm, bring some notes and review them as you sit on a recumbent bike or do the stair climber, rower, or elliptical. You'll end your session feeling charged from the workout while also lowering your stress level because you made progress on an important task.

Remember, Exercise Should Be Fun

Keep in mind, too, that you can exercise in ways that are both fun and functional. If you're super stressed-out, grab some friends for a quick game of basketball, Ultimate Frisbee, volleyball, or disc golf. You can socialize and get some exercise in at the same time. If you and a friend struggle to find time to spend together, sign up for an exercise class through the campus recreation center. You'll help each other stick to your commitment, have some time to catch up, and get a great workout in to boot.

⊗ Straight from a Student: Finding Time to Work Out

Nihar Suthar, a sophomore at Cornell University in New York, had been physically active before heading to college. Although he was worried about balancing his desire to exercise with his other obligations, he utilized a smart approach: Instead of worrying about finding hours to exercise, he focused instead on exactly how much time he did have. "I made it a habit," he says, "to always play tennis (on the days I had a lot of time) at our college courts, go to the gym (on days I had a decent amount of time), or just go for a short run (on days I didn't have a lot of time)."

Operating on the assumption that exercise would be part of his routine provided multiple benefits for Suthar. "I was able to get some sort of exercise in every single day and stayed very healthy," he notes. "Not only that, but exercising eliminated lots of my stress by clearing my mind from everything going on and provided me with a short, fun break to keep me focused on my work. I realized a difference in also how energetic and recharged I felt after exercising—making me more productive and getting me better grades overall. It was really a great strategy." Suthar's approach of focusing on exercising every day, in whatever time you have—instead of whether or not you will exercise—can be a great way to ensure you get your workout in, engage in some social time, and reduce your stress along the way.

Join an Intramural Team

One smart way to incorporate regular exercise is to join an intramural team. Unlike the official sports teams at your school, intramurals are more focused on enjoying the sport than winning victories. They can be a great way to meet more people, get some exercise, build some social connections, find mentors, make some friends, find potential roommates, meet potential significant others, and—perhaps most importantly—just have fun.

An Easy Place to Start: Yoga

If you're looking for a way to incorporate exercise—and all of its benefits, including stress reduction—into your college life, consider taking a yoga class.

"Yoga can be a college student's best friend," advises Grace Flowers, yoga instructor and founder of The OM Project. "It's there when you need some space, some alone time, some breathing time, some tuning in time and when you're finished letting it all go post practice, you feel so much better."

Because of yoga's popularity, you likely can find a class at your campus health and recreation center. If that's not an option, consider looking for one at a local gym, YMCA, private studio, or community organization. And if you still can't find one, chances are at least one person on your campus has at least a little experience teaching yoga; see if you can find enough students to form a class on your own.

Like other forms of exercise, yoga can provide lots of benefits—especially during your time in school. With the ups and downs of college classes, relationships, finances, and other stressors, engaging in a health-based, consistent form of exercise like yoga can help provide a sense of balance and the skills you need to keep your focus—and your stress levels—in check.

Solution #2: Sleep!

It's a rare college student who would pass on the opportunity to catch up on sleep. Sleep in college often takes place in a noisy apartment building or residence hall—or even in a noisy room—and happens at infrequent, irregular intervals. It's no wonder so many college students answer, "I'm tired!" when asked how they're doing.

Although college students view many common, sleep-related habits as normal—pulling all-nighters, for example—not getting enough sleep in college can wreak havoc on your ability to manage your classes, responsibilities, and stress.

You already know that sleep is important. You also probably already know that you feel and function much better when you're well rested. But it can be all too easy to let your sleep needs fall by the wayside when you're faced with mounting assignments, fun people, and all kinds of other situations that present themselves if you just stay up another thirty or sixty or ninety minutes.

You might even be able to convince yourself that you study better when you're pulling an all-nighter. But how much material will you really retain, after all, if you try to study while you're dozing off? How long will you stare at a blank laptop screen before finally getting a paragraph or two out? Trying to work when you're tired is like trying to go for a run when you haven't eaten. It just doesn't work well—if at all. You can go through the motions, but you end up not really doing what you're supposed to be doing. And after all your exhausting efforts, you're likely to find yourself even more tired and even more stressed, yet with little to show for it.

Figure Out How Much Sleep You Need

Being in college doesn't change the sleep requirements your body has. You need to sleep regularly, and enough, if you're going to function like a normal human being. Sleep may be easy to pass on, but it can be incredibly difficult to function without.

Getting enough sleep in college requires both a proactive and reactive approach. Just because everyone else around you is always tired doesn't mean you have to operate that way. A few simple tricks can help you keep your sleep—and, consequently, your stress—at appropriate levels.

Try to be as proactive as possible in figuring out how much sleep you need. Do you need seven hours? Eight? Nine? Remember to ask yourself what you need to function and think properly, not what you can get by on. Many students end up sleeping a vastly different number of hours from day to day—a few hours one night, then twelve the next. Getting your ideal amount of sleep each night is likely an unrealistic expectation, especially given that getting quality sleep can sometimes be out of your control (think: noisy party down the hall). Instead of worrying about each night, take a broader look at your sleep habits. How much do you ideally need? Are you getting that amount more often than not? If not, why not? And how can you aim to get the right amount of sleep on a more regular basis?

You might find that letting yourself sleep an extra thirty or sixty minutes a night ends up helping you get more done, not less. If you're able to think more clearly, function more effectively, and overall operate in a productive manner, you can easily save the time you spent sleeping through your efficiency. Additionally, your performance in other areas of your college life might improve. Just because your body is awake and ready for an exam doesn't mean your mind is.

Get More Sleep via Time Management

Just like any other obligation—to yourself, to your classes, to your financial situation—sleep is an appointment you need to keep. Consequently, put it in your calendar and don't let it be compromised except on rare occasions. While you may need to finish a paper or study a little bit more at the last minute, leading you to miss out on sleep, do your best to avoid sacrificing sleep as a result of poor time management. Aim to stay on top of your reading, work a little each day on major assignments, and overall feel in control of your classes and homework instead of vice versa.

Ask yourself questions about your sleep as you look at your calendar. Are you, for example, assuming you'll have to pull an all-nighter next week right before your midterm? If you can plan in advance to cram, you can just as easily plan in advance to study and rest. Be wise about the choices you make and realize when you're inadvertently setting yourself up for a stress-inducing, sleep-depriving situation.

Listen to Your Body

If you feel yourself getting sleepy during a busy day, try to stop things before they get worse. Consider taking a power nap for twenty minutes. You can rest just enough to recharge your body and mind while not sabotaging your attempts at a good night's sleep later.

Additionally, try to be as reactive as possible. Listen to what your body is telling you. Are you always tired? Are you not getting enough sleep on a regular basis? Are you sleeping through your morning classes a little too often? Your body has its sleep needs, regardless of whether it's finals week or the first week of class or summer vacation. Your job is to treat your body kindly and help it get the sleep it needs so that your mind can focus on the task at hand: being in college.

If you feel your body asking for more sleep, listen to it. It might be that you need more sleep more often, every day. Or it might be that your body is trying to fight off a virus and wants some extra rest so your immune system can do its job. It might be that your brain is so tired that it just needs some quiet time off. Whatever the reason, if you feel tired and are craving some high-quality shut-eye, get it. You just might surprise yourself with how much better you feel—and how much your stress decreases as a result.

Solution #3: Eat Healthy

Making smart choices about what you choose to eat—and when—can be one of the biggest challenges you face when it comes to managing your physical health and, consequently, your physical stress. There might be unlimited ice cream in the dining hall, delivery options at all hours of the night, and cuisines and dishes you've never been exposed to before. All of these tasty treats can easily add up to some seriously unhealthy eating habits and the physical consequences that come with them.

Good nutrition, however, is paramount when it comes to a college student's physical health, according to Liz Josefsberg, Director of Brand Advocacy for Weight Watchers and a personal trainer in New York. "When you're in college, you might act as if your nutrition or your health is the last thing on your list of things to do. You'll see a lot more success if you flip that and make it your top priority," she advises.

As any college student knows, however, prioritizing healthy eating is easier said than done—or so you might think. Amidst the sea of unhealthy (and seemingly endless) food choices, however, you can learn to make decisions that are in the best interest of your body and overall physical health.

Take Matters Into Your Own Hands

If there aren't any—or aren't enough—healthy food choices available on your campus, you'll likely have to learn how to incorporate your own. If you don't see healthy options at your campus dining locations, ask if they can be included. Many dining halls have suggestion boxes you can use, or you can ask to talk to the chef. Instead of veggies sautéed in butter, for example, politely ask if they can start offering grilled vegetable sides. Whenever you grab a sandwich to go, make sure it has vegetables on it, grab a piece of fruit to go as well, or see if there's a vegetarian option to replace the greasy cheeseburger you usually get. Add veggies to your pizza, always eat fruit with breakfast, and choose a low-calorie caffeinated beverage (like tea) instead of something that looks like coffee but is actually a milkshake in disguise.

Additionally, having healthy choices available consistently back in your room is important. Simple, inexpensive ideas include:

- Fresh options like apples and baby carrots, which last for a long time.
- Whole-grain crackers, which will provide nutrition while also satisfying your late-night munchies.
- Microwave popcorn (the kind without loads of butter, that is), which is easy to make, is healthy, has a long shelf life, and can quickly satisfy your hunger if you need to sustain yourself until your next meal. Additionally, the smell of fresh popcorn has the uncanny ability to make everyone come from miles around, so it can be a great way to facilitate a nutritional—and social—break during a late-night study session.

Easily accessible, easily made staples can provide you with appropriate snacks and nutrition during your busy life on the go. These simple choices can help keep you fueled during the day and prevent you from becoming too hungry before you finally do have time to eat.

Remember, Food Is Brain Fuel

While smart food choices and good nutrition can help keep hunger at bay, there are larger benefits that can have a positive, long-term effect on your college success, too. Through her work, Josefsberg helps hundreds of people each week focus on eating better and becoming healthier. "I see how eating more fruits and vegetables, staying away from processed foods, giving up soda, and getting away from high-fat, high-salt, high-sugar foods can all help you perform at your physical and mental best." Additionally, she notes that unhealthy foods like these "are showing to have an addictive quality in most people. You're not functioning at your best when your brain is thinking really hard on how to get more of that food instead of how to get an A on a test."

Your body is a critical part of your college success, and eating healthy is a critical factor in ensuring that success. What you eat has a major impact—for better or worse—on everything from how you feel to how you perform on exams to how you manage your stress levels.

Solution #4: Practice Good Physical Self-Care

It takes more than sleep and exercise to take care of your physical self during college. With so many factors at play, learning how to practice self-care can be one of the best skills you learn. "Self-care" is an important yet relatively vague concept. It means taking care of you—just you—in the ways that you need, when you need them, how you need them, and through solutions that work best for you, personally.

Fortunately or unfortunately, college will undoubtedly present you with many opportunities to learn more about what your body needs and likes. When your immune system is run-down and you've been giving your all for a long time, your choices will catch up with you. The way you take care of your physical self can be both a cause and an effect of the stress in your college life.

✪ Straight from a Student: Self-Care

Sara Smits Wilson, a 2012 graduate of the University of Nebraska-Lincoln, knows herself and her stress habits well. "I'm very prone to stress," she says. To help manage it, she developed some individual, personalized go-to tips and tricks. She knows, for example, that heading outdoors is a stress-busting solution that works particularly well for her. "Be outside," she recommends. "Just enjoy it. Sit on the porch, take the long way back to your car, eat lunch on a bench. You won't regret it." Simple, personalized approaches like Wilson's can make a major impact on how you're feeling physically, mentally, and emotionally.

It can be easy to learn to recognize when you need more sleep or when you should be getting more exercise. It can be more difficult, however, to realize when you're just run-down or in need of a change. Practicing self-care helps you read between the lines and see what your body needs so that it can handle the physical stresses you put on it.

The best approach to self-care is simple and steady. Check in with yourself once or twice a week, perhaps while in the shower. How are you feeling—really feeling? Too tired? Okay? Eager for the week to be over? Excited about an upcoming cocurricular program you're involved in? Use those few quiet moments you get to yourself in the morning to run a systems check:

- How is your physical self doing?
- What do you need today to feel a little better, or to keep yourself feeling great? Should you maybe grab a granola bar on your way to class, even though you usually skip breakfast? Should you not be drinking so much coffee in the afternoons?
- Should you just make yourself go to your intramural rugby practice, even though you're on the fence about going? Will you feel better if you go—or worse?

Good self-care is important because *you* are the best at figuring out what it looks like for you as an individual. Learn to hear—and listen to—the smaller messages your body is communicating to you. The way you treat your body is going to influence your stress levels in college, just like your stress levels in college are going to influence your body. Pay special attention to the messages your body is giving you, whether big or small, frequent or infrequent. You need to learn to practice self-care because it's up to you now, as an independent adult, to monitor and promote your own physical health. And self-care is an important part of doing so.

Solution #5: Recognize the Physical Manifestations of Stress

As you learn to listen to your body, you'll likely learn to recognize the signs that the stress in your life is starting to manifest itself physically.

While stress presents itself differently in everyone—you might feel your shoulders becoming tight whereas your roommate might not be able to sleep well—the important thing is to focus on how the stress is having an effect on your physical health. Brynn Kimball, RN, BSN, who works in Cardiology Services at the University of Utah, and Grace

Flowers, yoga instructor and founder of The OM Project, note that the physical manifestations of stress can include:

- Sleep disturbances and/or fatigue
- Muscle tension or aches
- Headaches
- Changes in eating habits
- Lack of self-confidence
- Zits
- Dark circles under the eyes
- Stomachaches or digestion problems

There are several different approaches that can counteract the physical manifestations of stress while in college. You can treat the symptoms, you can treat the cause, or you can treat both.

Treating the Symptoms

Treating the symptoms can be more of a short-term solution, but that doesn't mean it's any less important. If you're feeling physically run-down, overwhelmed, or just not yourself and you think stress is the cause, treat yourself to a little TLC. The self-care now will pay off greatly down the road.

Relieving your physical stress doesn't have to be expensive or time consuming:

- If you're feeling lethargic…get outside and get some exercise, whether it's going for a long walk by yourself or playing a team sport with some friends. If the weather doesn't support an outside stress-reliever, consider taking a class, like yoga, in the campus gym or even doing some basic stretches in your room.

- If you're feeling tense…try a massage! If you can't afford a professional one, see if you can find a friend whose back you can rub for twenty minutes if he or she agrees to rub yours, too. Or, better yet, head to a mall that offers chair massages by the minute. Even a ten-minute massage by a trained therapist can do wonders.

- If you're feeling mentally exhausted…consider allowing yourself to mentally check out in a healthy way. Head to a museum and just enjoy yourself for an hour or two, without worrying about taking notes or studying the exhibits for an upcoming exam. Treat yourself to a magazine on a topic you find silly but fun. Get off campus and try something new, whether it's a new restaurant or some kind of community event. In essence: Let your mind escape from college for a little while so that your body can relax, too.

Treating the Causes

While treating the physical symptoms of stress can be helpful, treating the causes can be even more beneficial. Break down the basic sources of your physical stress. Are your tight shoulders caused by something easy to fix, like a really bad residence hall mattress? Buying something like an egg-crate mattress topper can be an inexpensive way to transform a bad bed, and thinking creatively about the physical discomforts in your life can lead you to some smart, effective, and fast solutions.

Other physical stressors, however, can be more complicated. Is your immune system run-down because you haven't been paying attention to your physical health? If this is the case, be your own best advocate.

Have a serious heart-to-heart conversation with yourself. What do you need to be doing better? Do you need to be sleeping more, eating healthier, getting more exercise? Do you need to let some obligations go, like cocurricular commitments? What advice would a mom give to someone like you in your situation? What advice would you give to a friend in your situation?

Instead of arguing with yourself, listen to yourself. Go to bed earlier, start making smarter food choices, work in thirty minutes of exercise a day, and focus on what your body needs to not feel so stressed-out all of the time. Slowly but surely, you're likely to see your stress melt away as you begin to focus on being healthy instead of feeling frustrated at how weary your body feels all the time.

Solution #6: Build Healthy Routines

There are endless reasons why you can't stick to a healthy routine. It's the first week of classes. It's Rush Week. You have a big game on Friday. It's your roommate's birthday. You have a big midterm coming up. The classmates in your group project totally dropped the ball, so now you have to do everything. You just have to finish your tasks before going home for the long weekend. It's midterms again. It's finals week.

By the end of the semester, however, this kind of approach leaves you with months of unhealthy choices. Your goals to exercise and eat better never really manifested, despite your best efforts. Your body assumes, by this point, that caffeine and energy drinks are the main staples of your diet.

Whether or not you are consciously choosing to create them, you already have healthy—or unhealthy—routines and habits in your life. If you never made it to the gym, for example, and always ate poorly throughout the semester, then that was your routine. Be it healthy or unhealthy, you definitely have a pattern of some kind.

While being mindful about your routines is a great way to start a new semester, you can always refocus and reprioritize yourself and your health if you feel things getting out of balance. Consider these questions:

- What has your routine been? What do you want it to be? Is there a difference between the two? If not, how can you keep yourself focused? If so, how can you bridge the gap?
- What kinds of things have been getting in the way of incorporating a healthy routine?
- What specific steps can you take to make your desired routine more of a reality?

If you're more likely to stick to something if it involves a commitment to others, sign up for an exercise class or make an appointment with a friend to meet at the gym on certain dates and times. Use your calendar and your support systems as a way to hold yourself accountable.

If you do best handling things on your own, put reminders in your calendar to eat fruits and vegetables with every meal and walk or bike to certain classes instead of driving or taking the bus. If you need help drawing boundaries around unhealthy behaviors, let your roommate know that you're going to be trying to get more sleep and that he or she needs to find somewhere else to hang out with friends on Thursday nights.

As simple as it sounds, it's true: The only person who can incorporate, and stick with, a healthy routine in your college life is you. Do your best to make it happen and keep trying, even if you keep hitting speed bumps.

An occasionally healthy routine is better than a blatantly unhealthy one, and you'll likely be rewarded with more energy, more focus, and much less stress every time you make progress. After all, you're going to have a routine one way or the other. So why not make it one that leaves you feeling great?

Solution #7: Find Yourself Some Personal Space

One of the larger challenges students who live on campus face is the lack of privacy. You are likely never by yourself during the day—or even at night. You probably have a roommate, roommates, or a suite full of people you live with. Your residence hall buzzes with sound and activity at all hours, and you aren't even alone when you're in the bathroom. And while you may love the community aspect of being in college, all that community can sometimes be overwhelming.

Can You Be Alone Anywhere?

It can be very challenging to try to make your own, personalized, personal, stress-free space in a college environment. The physical structures of college seem to always be against you: shared rooms, shared residence halls, shared classrooms, shared event spaces. Everywhere you go, you're expected to be with other people. And yet sometimes the best way to reduce your stress is to be by yourself.

One important aspect to consider when trying to manage your stress is to think about where, physically, you can actually deal with it. Where can you go to get some time alone? Where can you really relax and not hear a lot of background noise? Where can you look around and see just trees and sky instead of lecture halls, students with backpacks, and the overall hustle and bustle of campus?

Learning how to make and claim your own physical space is an important skill to learn when it comes to tackling the stress in your life. Doing stress-relieving activities with your friends is of course smart, but making a date with yourself can also be helpful.

Visit Busy Spots at Off-Peak Times

Trying to find your own, private, physical space—and the privacy that accompanies it—can indeed be challenging. One of the best approaches you can take when trying to carve out your own quiet place on campus is to go to busy places at nontraditional times.

Your room, for example, is probably a relatively busy space. Your roommate might be home most of the evenings, when you two do homework and hang out with friends. If so, think about heading to your room midmorning or midafternoon, when the halls are relatively quiet and your roommate, for example, is in lab for a few hours.

Similarly, think about the places you spend the busiest times of your day. The dining hall, food court, and food stations around campus all get incredibly busy around dinner and lunch. Consider, then, heading there for a little quiet time in the early morning, in the middle of the afternoon, or even after the dinner rush. You can have a quiet meal with just yourself (or even a calming friend) and enjoy a new space that you've reinvented.

The Importance of Quiet

You just might surprise yourself at how much having a quiet space can help reduce your stress. After all, when was the last time you were in a place that didn't have some kind of background noise? That wasn't visually busy? That didn't have bright lights and flashing screens? Letting your senses calm down can do wonders for your stress levels and relaxation, even if you're only able to escape for a few moments. It's definitely worth it.

Additionally, even though your entire campus might feel like it's busy all the time, only certain parts of it are busy all of the time. Just like your residence hall is relatively quiet during the day, certain buildings on campus have peak times, too. To avoid them:

- Head to a seminar room during lunch if you want some quiet space; you'll likely find one that's not in use and will discover a quiet nook where you can just relax for a bit.
- Peek into a large lecture hall when it's empty or find a small conference area in an academic building.
- Reserve your own carrel in the library; you can, of course, use it to study, but you can also use it to just relax and clear your mind.

There are lots of secret spaces like these you can find when you need your own private corner of the world to help keep things in perspective.

Solution #8: Stay Healthy (Even in a Residence Hall)

Living in a residence hall can be one of the best experiences of your time in college. The people, the community, the activities, and the ridiculousness that take place there will be something you remember for years to come. The shared community can also be a great resource for helping you maintain your commitment to physical health and stress reduction.

While you'll likely be grateful for the memories you'll share with your hall mates, you probably would happily pass on the shared germs. As fun as residence halls can be, they can also wreak havoc on your ability to stay healthy. Similar to how sleep, nutrition, and exercise can be important parts of your physical health and battle against physical stress, being healthy in a residence hall should be an important part of the equation. All of the little choices you make—for good or for bad—add up to larger consequences.

Just like in any communal situation (including even hospitals), you have to be mindful about taking extra care of your physical health when living in a residence hall. This is not to say that residence halls are dirty by nature or a bad place to live, but there are steps you should take when you live anywhere with a lot of other people who share a bathroom and living space.

Bathroom Hygiene

What worked in your home before you went to college might not be a good idea once you're in a residence hall. Leaving your toothbrush in the residence hall bathroom, for example: bad idea. In fact, even if your bathroom has a little space you can use to store your things, it might be best to keep your toiletries in your room so you can be more in charge of what (and whom) they come in contact with.

Similarly, be smart with your bathroom habits:

- Always wash your hands.
- Wear shower shoes.
- Remember to wash your towel whenever you do laundry.
- Clean up when you're done with your things so you don't accidentally leave your razor out in the open for two days, where other people can use it and knock it on the floor and overall get it dirty without your noticing.

Keep Yourself as Germ-Free as Possible

While it's important to be nice and share when appropriate, it's also okay to keep some things to yourself. Don't share cups or drinks, for example.

If you have a friend who wants to hang out even though he or she is clearly getting sick, see if you can head somewhere outside—or at least somewhere other than your room. And if you know that, say, a bad cold is slowly working its way through your residence hall, pay extra attention to your sleep, eating, and exercise habits so that your immune system can do its job.

Solution #9: Have a Healthy—and Changing—Self-Image

It would be unfortunate if you graduated from college with the exact same self-image you had when you first started. Even if your self-image is completely healthy, your understanding of yourself should deepen and grow. And if your self-image is unhealthy, you can ideally learn more about where that perspective comes from—and how to conquer it.

How Physical Changes Have an Impact on Self-Image

College is a time of intense growth in all kinds of ways, and part of that growth will influence how you see yourself. There might be physical changes, too, that have an impact on your self-image:

- You might gain some weight; you might lose some weight. (You might do both!)

- You might exercise less than you did in high school; you might exercise a lot more.
- You might feel your body changing as you physically grow from a teenager to a young adult.
- You might start to feel—and physically notice—the effects that some of your behaviors, both positive and negative, are having on your body.

All of these factors will undoubtedly influence, for better or worse, your self-image. As difficult as it can be, however, keep in mind that, as you work so hard in your classes to learn new things and expand how you intellectually approach new ideas, you will also have to work on learning how to view yourself in new (and even exciting) ways.

Manage Your Self-Image in a Healthy Way

"Every person, whether in college or not, deals with self-image and body image conflicts," notes Brynn Kimball, RN, BSN, who works in Cardiology Services at the University of Utah, "and everyone uses effective and ineffective coping strategies." The important thing is knowing how to tell the difference and making sure your coping strategies stay positive and effective. "Ineffective coping strategies like withdrawing, substance abuse, eating disorders, acting aggressively, or suicidal thoughts can become addictive or even fatal. Learning effective coping strategies to deal with stress is important and will last a lifetime," she adds.

Similarly, Kimball says, "With effective coping, you will learn how to explore and clarify your feelings and identify and take control of your thoughts; while getting support, you can verbalize your feelings and thoughts with someone you trust. It's also important to trust your feelings and know they are valid...Focus on the present, stay with facts, and be optimistic and realistic in your expectations." The way you view yourself may change and grow during your time in school, but it's important to focus on your self-image as a part of your healthy, health-based college identity rather than another stressor in an already stressful context.

As you work to both prevent and reduce the stress in your college life, aim to treat your physical self in a way that is positive and health-based. With so much else going on, the last thing you need to do is give yourself more to stress about. Your beautiful brain, after all, is part of your physical body, and keeping all parts of yourself healthy is key to doing well during your time in school.

Practice Positive Self-Talk

Part of your self-image includes how you talk to yourself. Even if you think no one can hear the harsh words you might internally say to yourself about what you should improve on, what you did wrong, and what others are thinking about you, there is one person who hears everything: you. And if you wouldn't tolerate someone else talking to you the way that you talk to yourself, then don't let yourself get away with it.

Celebrate Yourself!

Having a healthy self-image means appreciating all that you do right and all the great things your body lets you accomplish. Celebrate those achievements, whether they're as basic as getting to class on time or as impressive as acing your Japanese Painting final. You have enough to stress about while in college; don't add on unnecessary stressors by being too harsh on yourself. Let your self-image grow into something that helps you realize the amazing, strong person you are.

A Word about Alcohol and Stress

It's no secret that college culture can sometimes facilitate unhealthy drinking habits. And given that alcohol can also reduce your ability to make wise, health-based choices, it's also no secret that poor alcohol behaviors can greatly contribute to the stress you experience during college.

If you're going to drink in college, be smart about it. Seemingly inconsequential choices can, in fact, have major and long-term consequences. Your decision to sneak some beers into your residence hall room might lead to your being placed on probation for violating residence hall rules. A simple twist of fate can transform those few beers you thought would help you relax into a major source of stress.

Similarly, your choice to drink a little bit too much one night might lead to your inability to make it to class on time the next day, to make it to your work shift on time, or to perform well on an important exam. And since alcohol has an effect on your decision-making skills, you might easily end up making choices that you otherwise would shy away from—choices that can have serious and long-term consequences for your mental, emotional, and physical health.

If you want to use alcohol to relax, that's okay. (As long as you're of legal age, of course.) Just use it wisely and make sure it's a small part of other ways you have to relax—say, a nice glass of wine during dinner with friends or a celebratory beer after your rugby win—instead of the *only* way to relax. You work hard to do well in school, to keep your stress in check, and to make the most of the opportunities you have. Don't let poor alcohol choices and unwise alcohol behaviors sabotage all that you've accomplished.

Physical Stress: Conclusion and Highlights

Your physical life is demanding, and with everything else you have going on, it's no wonder that some of your stressors begin manifesting themselves in physical ways. Ideally, you can learn to prevent physical stress before it happens. If not, learning to deal with it is equally as important. A holistic approach works best when your efforts are intentional, part of a routine, and based on smart choices.

- **When your physical health is suffering from stress, start with the basics.** Incorporate exercise into your schedule, even if it's only a little bit each day. Sign up for a class, plan a workout appointment with a friend, or incorporate exercise in other parts of your routine. Additionally, make sure you get enough sleep on a regular basis and eat as healthy as possible, whenever possible.
- **Remember that part of your independence involves being responsible for your own self-care.** It's up to you to monitor what you eat, when you exercise, how much sleep you get, and overall how you approach taking care of your physical self. Prioritizing what your body needs instead of what you can get by on is a helpful way to keep stress at bay or handle it when it inevitably presents itself.
- **Prioritize your physical health in your routines.** Eating well one week (or day) won't counteract the stress you're already carrying around, and it definitely won't help you deal with the stress you'll face as the semester progresses. Think about how you can incorporate wise, health-based choices into your schedule so that being healthy and preventing stress become your routine. Otherwise, not

taking care of yourself and feeling stressed-out all the time may become your routine by default.

- **Find some alone time.** Your time in college is likely spent around a lot of other people. Learn where and how you can carve out time to let your mind relax and sort through the stress you're facing. Find places that support your relaxation instead of trying to decompress in an environment that is always full of people and activity. Similarly, if you live in a residence hall, be aware of the challenges that communal living presents to your physical health—and stress levels. Just like you would anywhere else, make wise choices about taking care of your things and your body in a health-based way.
- **It's okay if your body image and self-image change and grow during your time in college.** Do your best to view yourself as a positive, productive, worthy, healthy individual. Don't talk to yourself in a way you wouldn't permit others to; doing so just adds unnecessary stress to your life. Be your own best advocate instead of your own worst enemy. And be patient with yourself as you learn and grow and change during your college journey.
- **If you choose to consume alcohol during your time in school, do so wisely.** If you'd like to use alcohol to help reduce or alleviate some of your stress, make smart choices about how you make this happen. Alcohol can be an aid to stress reduction, but it should not be the main mechanism for doing so. Additionally, be aware of how alcohol can inhibit wise decision-making and can quickly, if unintentionally, become a source of stress.

CHAPTER 5

Social Stress

If you were to ask high school students what they see when they close their eyes and picture college, they probably would have more nonacademic visions than not. Scenes of life in the residence hall, weekend parties, sports events, fraternities and sororities, and general social times with friends feature prominently in the minds of many students—and with good reason.

College is, after all, an amazing opportunity for you to meet new people. Your school likely has students in attendance from across the country and around the world. There are people who have interests, religions, political views, cultures, habits, and traditions that you might never have encountered before. You might also find, perhaps for the first time, large numbers of people who share your own values and beliefs. College can truly be a once-in-a-lifetime opportunity when looking at the social benefits alone.

Conversely, of course, college can also present you with new, unique, and difficult challenges when it comes to the social scene. Learning to balance seemingly endless social plans, constantly being challenged to step outside of your social comfort zone, and working to find a place where you truly fit in can quickly turn the social side of college into a major stressor. So just what can you do to make sure the social aspect of your college life stays a fun and positive part of your college experience—instead of a stressful one?

Social Stress: Identifying the Sources

The social scene in college presents an interesting challenge for students, as the very same situations that might ideally help you relieve stress—such as hanging out with friends—can suddenly become sources of stress if, for example, you haven't made good friends yet.

Social Stress: The Five Questions

1. *In general, how would I describe my college social life at this point in time?* If you were to think of five adjectives that describe your college social life, what words come to mind? How do you feel, overall, about your social life? What kinds of friendships do you have? What kinds of social experiences are you having? What kinds of relationships are you forming? How might others describe your social life? Generally speaking, does your social scene add stress to your college life? Reduce stress? Both? How?

2. *Is my social life what I was expecting it to be?* If so, how is it the same? If not, how is it different? Are you happy with the ways your social life is turning out? Do you wish it had turned out the way you planned? Do you wish it had turned out differently? What major choices did you make that have formed your social life? Are you enjoying your social life overall? If so, what in particular do you find enjoyable? If not, what in particular is proving less enjoyable than what you had hoped? Are you challenging yourself socially in ways that are healthy? If not, why not?

3. *In what positive ways is my social life contributing to my college experience?* How is your social life enhancing, adding to,

or otherwise improving your time in college? What kinds of things have you experienced or learned through your social involvement that you are grateful for? How has your social life helped you grow and learn? How has it helped you develop new skills? What parts of your social life have been the most beneficial to you? What kinds of activities and involvement can you not imagine being without now? What has been your best social experience so far during your time in school? How have the benefits of your social life helped prevent or reduce your stress?

4. *In what negative ways is my social life contributing to my college experience?* What has been the biggest challenge for you thus far, when it comes to the college social scene? What have you not enjoyed? What have you regretted? What kinds of things would you like to remove from your social sphere? What kinds of things are you grateful to have done but now need to let go? What aspects of your social life, and perhaps the college social scene in general, add stress to your life? How can you remove these aspects so you are less stressed in the future?

5. *Would I like to change anything about my college social life?* If so, what? What top three things could you think of that you might want to alter, even if only a little bit? Why would you want to make these changes? Would making these changes add or reduce your stress levels? What could you substitute that will provide more positive, healthy social experiences during your time in school?

Finding Solutions

The social scene in college is unlike any other aspect of your college life. Because of its unique importance and challenges, it becomes even more essential for you to pause and ask yourself some critical questions about what your social life is contributing—positively or negatively—to your college experience.

Solution #1: Understand the College Social Scene

Colleges and universities are living, breathing spaces that are constantly in a state of change. There are always, always things going on; even if it's 2:00 A.M. and things are quiet in the main quad, there's undoubtedly a heated debate going on in a residence hall lobby somewhere and students giggling from exhaustion as they try to stay up late studying for an important exam. Even two roommates quietly doing their reading are contributing to the social community of the campus, whether it's by sharing a pot of coffee or letting a friend study in the room with them.

A college's social scene is defined by how a campus community interacts with itself. What do students do when they're not focused on academic pursuits? What kinds of activities, programs, and other events go on after hours? What do people do when they get together to just hang out? What do people do when they need to relax? In essence: What makes up the what, when, where, who, why, and how of your campus social dynamics?

The What

If you want to figure out the basics of your college social scene, take a twenty-minute walk around campus and look at what's being advertised. You'll likely see flyers for parties, cultural celebrations, quad events, and volunteer opportunities. Some student groups may be advertising for an upcoming event with sidewalk chalk. Fraternities and sororities might have hung banners, trying to recruit students for their next pledge class. Academic-based clubs and organizations might be letting people know about their next meetings.

Take a moment and digest exactly what has a social presence on your campus:

- What kinds of things are going on?
- What kinds of groups are trying to reach out to you?
- What kinds of people are making an effort to make your campus a more fun and social place?
- Perhaps most importantly, what are you naturally drawn to?

Understanding your role in the "what" on your campus is important when it comes to managing your college stress. After all, if you can find a group or activity or program or volunteer initiative that you absolutely love, it will likely contribute greatly to your social happiness—and to your stress reduction. If, for example, you really connect with people in your Women in Science club, you are more likely to hang out with them during social events, go to speakers together, network together, and even possibly live together in a year or two when several of you decide to move off campus. Connecting with people in a social way is important for your health and happiness, and finding out what's going on is a great way to figure out where to go to make those connections happen.

The When

One thing that can frequently be overlooked when trying to connect and understand your campus's social scene is the "when." While what happens is important, when things happen is also important. If you know, for example, that you are always going to have to be up early for track practice, joining a fraternity or sorority that has frequent late-night events might not be a great fit. Similarly, if you work at night, trying to connect with social groups that meet during the day is a smart idea. You don't, after all, want to add more complications—and more stress—to your life by adding unnecessary scheduling conflicts to your to-do list. While finding what's right for you is important, remember that finding things that happen during a time that's right for you is important, too.

Make sure to leave yourself time in your schedule to actually have a social life. Just like you don't want to unintentionally become involved with social activities and commitments that conflict with your schedule, you don't want to unintentionally create a schedule that has no time at all for social involvement.

✪ **Straight from a Student:**
Finding Time for a Social Life

Josh Swedlund, a sophomore at Northern Michigan University, came up with a unique approach that works perfectly for him. He realized that, after a long day of going to class, working, and being involved with clubs and other activities, he was pretty wiped. However, he felt a tension between needing to work on his homework when he got home and wanting to have a social life. He realized that, while trying to do homework at night might be a smart way to go about his daily schedule, it was also a sure way to increase his stress.

Swedlund then came up with a solution that works great for his own preferences and abilities: He wakes up very early in the morning to do his homework. "I wake up every morning at 5:30 (with the help of coffee, of course), and being conscious of my roommate so I don't wake him up with a noisy alarm," he says. "This way, I can come back from class after a long day, relax, and de-stress with social time, while setting aside time in the morning to finish homework. I find that at 5:30, everyone is asleep, and homework can be done in a study lounge/lobby/hallway without interruption and with complete silence."

Even though this solution may not work for everyone, Swedlund found a creative solution that works for him. The takeaway: His solution both provides more social time and reduces his stress levels. "Before I started waking up early, I was actually falling asleep while trying to take notes for class and that is a horrible idea, to say the least," he jokes. "Stress would build in class when I couldn't understand my own notes or miss important details." Now, however, his technique of waking up early "works for me and my body, and helps add a couple of hours of relaxation to my schedule for after classes."

The Where

Spaces on a college campus often serve one specific function. Academic buildings, for example, are rarely the site of late-night campus parties, while residence hall lobbies can be difficult to use exclusively for academic-based events.

These kinds of dynamics, however, can prove quite useful to you as you try to figure out the "where" of your campus social scene. Where do you spend most of your time? Where would you like to spend more time? Are there things going on in certain places—say, on a certain part of campus—that you seem to be drawn to? Do you just like some parts of campus better than others? The answers to these questions can help you figure out where, physically, you feel most at home in a social sense. It could be that you love a certain coffee shop so much because you connect with the type of people who hang out there. Or it could be that, because you're spending so much time in lab, you're naturally connecting in a social way with the other students who are there late at night, too.

Understanding the "where" of the college social scene can help you figure out where best to spend your social time. If you are frequently finding yourself alone in your room, you likely aren't experiencing all you could be when it comes to the social side of school. Instead, head out of your room to where you feel most comfortable. Whether it's the quad, the lobby in an academic building, a common area in a beautiful new library, or a coffee shop, you're much more likely to organically start a conversation—and perhaps even a friendship—with someone in these kinds of social, public places than you are alone in your room.

In essence, knowing where you physically feel most at home and most comfortable on your campus can help you figure out where you can start building up and connecting with social support systems. And having strong social support systems, of course, can do wonders for reducing your stress throughout your time in school.

The Who

One of the most amazing aspects of being in college is the opportunity you have to connect with all kinds of people from all walks of life. Colleges are usually quite intentional about bringing in a diverse student body, specifically so everyone has the chance to learn from each other—both inside and outside of the classroom.

When trying to figure out the social scene and how you fit in, think about the kinds of people you most enjoy being around. Do you find comfort in hanging out with students who are very similar to yourself? Do you enjoy learning from people with whom you seemingly have nothing in common? Are there a few people you met during orientation with whom you felt you had a strong connection? Is there a certain club, fraternity or sorority, or sports team that you find yourself naturally drawn to?

Just like your time before college, the people with whom you interact with socially are a huge part of your life. The friends you make, the clubs you join, and the social circles you participate in all have a major impact on your experience (not to mention your stress levels). It's important, then, to figure out what kinds of people you want to be around.

College can be a great place to make a fresh start and to try to step outside of your comfort zones if you want to shake things up. If, for example, you've never checked out theater groups before but would like to, go for it. Look for people and groups who are smart, kind, generous, and—of course—fun. There's really no reason why college can't be one of the most amazing experiences for you as a person. With so many people involved in so many things, it's up to you to choose what you'd like. Choose what kinds of people you want to be around and go from there.

The Why and the How

Unfortunately, that simple act of making friends can sometimes seem overwhelming. If you find that to be the case, you're not alone. If you're new to college, there's practically no limit on how many opportunities you'll have to meet new people. Orientation events, the first day of classes, the first meetings of clubs and organizations, club fairs, intramural sports team practices, events in your residence hall, and even random barbecues in the quad can all provide a chance for you to walk up to someone (or a group of people) new to you and introduce yourself. Those thirty seconds of bravery can literally transform your life.

Remember, too, that everyone is new in college in some way or another. New classes start. New students join clubs. New clubs are formed. New students transfer in. A new roommate arrives into your residence hall. A new friendship starts between people in a class.

Because of this, the rules for meeting people in college aren't necessarily the same as they are everywhere else. It's totally normal to introduce yourself to people all the time. You might be at a party in the middle of the semester when someone walks up to your group and says "hello." Maybe this person knows someone in your circle and just walked over to talk and hang out. You wouldn't think of that as strange; that's just what people do in a college community.

Similarly, while it may feel awkward at first, your approaching a group of people isn't strange, either. And you just might surprise yourself at how much easier it is than you thought. (Even if the group includes the cutie you've noticed in your comparative politics class…) Try to think of something simple to say as a way to break the ice, such as mentioning a class you have in common, or asking a question about the event you're all attending.

Instead of serving as a cause of stress, connecting with people in college can ideally help you alleviate stress. You never know who might end up being a dear friend, who might end up being a great tennis partner, who might share your passion for gaming, who might be a whiz at a subject you're struggling with, who might be your roommate next year, or who might be the love of your life. The only way to find any of this out is to take a deep breath, be brave, and do your best to reach out and connect with people in as many social ways as possible. You can do it!

Solution #2: Find Social Groups with Expectations and Habits That Match Yours

Once you make the leap and start talking with people, you might find yourself being pulled in multiple directions. Do you want to go with your quadmates to see a friend's band perform? Do you want to see the dance production that your friend is involved in? Do you want to go out and grab pizza with your lab partners after a long week of work? Do you just want to stay in with your significant other and stream cheesy movies all night?

One important thing to keep in mind as you try to connect with different people and groups is to be intentional about your college experience. Close your eyes, take a few deep breaths, and imagine yourself thirty years from now:

- What do you want your social memories of college to be like? What do you want to look back on and smile about?
- What kinds of experiences do you want to make sure to have?
- What kinds of things might you view as a waste of time?
- What might you regret doing? What might you regret not doing?

There's a strong correlation between your social involvement and your stress levels. If you are forming friendships, are enjoying your school's social scene (in whichever ways are best for you), are feeling connected with people, and overall feel like you belong socially at your school, you're much more likely to be able to better deal with—and even prevent—stress in other areas of your college life. Conversely, if your social life is adding stress to your experience, you're much more likely to not enjoy yourself in other areas and to find yourself struggling with the things that are the most fundamental and important—like your academics.

Be Yourself

It's critical to find social groups that have expectations and habits that match your own. If you like to go to bed early, for example, that's perfectly fine! But joining a group of friends who mock you for your early bedtimes, who constantly pressure you to stay out late, or who otherwise don't support what you need to do to take care of yourself is a recipe for disaster. While you may technically have friends and be involved, you might not be doing so in a way that is positive and healthy.

Thirty years from now, you might in fact feel very silly if you looked back at your college years and saw yourself trying to please a group of people who didn't seem to understand what made you, well, *you*. In essence, your social life in college should support you as a unique individual. Do you like to go out late at night, hearing new underground bands? Do you like to participate in sports, traveling with a team? Do you like to belong to a fraternity or sorority, thereby having access to a broad social network while also contributing to a larger community? Do you like to just have one or two close friends with whom you can stay up late talking?

There's no right or wrong way to interact with the social scene in college; it's just what's right or wrong *for you*. If you love the party scene and think the weekend starts on Wednesday night, go for it. (As long as you stay afloat in your classes, of course.) If you hate the party scene and instead want to read and write poetry on a Saturday afternoon with some friends, that's fantastic, too—because it's what you want and need in a social sense, and what makes you the person that you are.

Some Social Stress Is Okay

Your social involvement will undoubtedly have some correlation to the stress you feel during your time in school. The key, however, is to make sure that the social stress you feel is healthy. Feeling stressed about being overly involved and not having enough time to do your homework is a bad kind of stress. But feeling a little stressed and anxious about assuming a leadership role in your club or organization is a good kind of stress. The former doesn't support your growth, either academically or socially, whereas the latter challenges you in a positive way to step outside of your comfort zone, learn new skills, and meet new people.

Solution #3: Always Look to Expand Your Social Scene

During the first few weeks of classes, everyone is busy putting all the pieces of their semester or quarter in place. Moving in, getting settled, registering for classes, buying books, and establishing a general routine takes a few weeks. During that time, nearly every student group on campus is reaching out to find new members, whether it's the Quidditch Club, the Black Student Alliance, or even student government.

Joining Groups Midsemester

Once the dust settles and you're a few weeks or even months into the academic year, you might suddenly realize that you'd like to join a particular club or look more into something like the student newspaper. Unfortunately, many students assume that once the initial start-of-the-semester window passes, it's practically impossible for students to join new social circles. You might be thinking: *The groups don't want new members; everyone is already friends. It'd be awkward to go to a meeting; I don't know anyone there; they probably already have enough people involved anyway.*

In reality, however, it's a rare student group or social clique that isn't interested in—if not actively looking for—new members. Don't let your worries about what might happen prevent what could happen.

- If you want to join a club but aren't sure if it's open to people popping in midsemester, just e-mail the president and ask.
- If you want to work for the newspaper but think they might be full, see if you can contribute an opinion piece or two.
- If you just realize that you have more time than you think and still want to be involved in the fall musical production, ask how you can volunteer.

Feeling stressed or anxious about being rejected is usually unfounded in situations like these. Everyone in college knows what it's like to want to be involved, to want to contribute, and to want to connect. Reaching out and trying to do so is likely to be rewarded, not shunned.

Starting Your Own Group

Additionally, if you're realizing that you're not quite finding the community you had hoped for, gather your courage, head to the student activities office (or your campus equivalent, which may be called a student leadership or student engagement office), and ask how to start a club of your own. Chances are, even on the smallest of campuses, you're likely not the only person who has an interest that's not being met. Starting your own club or organization can be a great way to meet new people, become more involved socially, and add a missing piece to your campus community. Even if only two or three other people express an interest, you've at least met two or three other people with whom you share something in common.

Preferring a Quiet Social Life Is Okay, Too

It's okay if you prefer to have a rather uneventful, quiet social life during your time in school. Some students are so outgoing and friendly that they could have a conversation and make friends with a brick wall. Others are more introverted and enjoy quieter, simpler social activities and connections. Trying to be one type of student when you're really the other only puts you in a stress-inducing, uncomfortable, unsustainable situation. The most important part of your college social life is to keep challenging yourself in new and healthy ways. There's a big difference, however, between pushing yourself to grow and pushing yourself to become someone you're not.

Solution #4: Find Social Circles That Support Your Academics

One important aspect to keep in mind is that your social life in college should complement your academics, not detract from them.

Amidst the hustle and bustle of your busy social life, your academics can easily get lost in the mix. You might plan to catch up on your reading once Rush Week is over, but when that week finally ends, you find yourself pledging the fraternity or sorority you hoped to join. While this can be exactly what you wanted, it might not provide you with what you needed: the time to catch up on your classes and stay on top of your homework and reading.

Finding a Balance Is an Ongoing Challenge

Balancing your social life and your academic obligations is a difficult thing to master—and because your college life is constantly moving, you won't one day wake up and suddenly be able to meet all of your obligations. One week, you'll feel like you're spending too much social time with your friends; the next week, you'll feel like your classes have taken over your life as you study for midterms. Both are okay as long as, at the end of the semester, you've done well in your classes and had some fun along the way. Keeping academics as your highest priority during your time in school doesn't necessarily mean that you pass on every fun opportunity that presents itself; it simply means that you make sure your social obligations and involvement are complementary to your academic obligations.

Despite your best efforts, there will be times when your academics and your social life come into conflict with each other; it's just a part of being in college. When that happens, it's important to be patient with yourself. It might be frustrating to not be able to do everything you want socially, just as it can be frustrating to not be able to meet all of your academic requirements despite your best efforts.

In these kinds of situations, it's a smart idea to check in with yourself and make sure that the conflict is an exception to the rule and not the rule itself. Overall, do your friends and activities help you resolve the situation when your academics conflict with your social life? Do they put pressure on you to prioritize in ways you're not comfortable with, or do they ask how they can help? In essence: Is your social sphere supportive of your academics? Having the two in conflict every once in a while is just a part of being in school. But having them in conflict all of the time is a sure way to add a lot of difficult yet preventable stress into your life.

Learning Outside the Classroom

Your learning process in college takes on all kinds of forms. Most students would agree that learning doesn't only happen in a lecture hall, seminar room, or lab. Some of the best college "aha!" moments are those that happen spontaneously, like during a philosophical debate in a residence hall lounge or during a group study session. Your social life can complement your academics in the sense that interacting with intelligent, interesting people helps you think and learn in different ways. An added benefit is that you'll have fun—and often reduce your stress—during the process in a way that doesn't always happen inside a classroom.

Your more formal social involvement—say, assuming a leadership role in a club or serving in student government—can also complement your academic learning. The skills you gain, after all, by organizing a large event, leading a team, responding to an important political issue, or providing vision for a group of people are incredibly important. You might find a practical way to apply the marketing skills you're learning in class by advertising an upcoming, large-scale campus program you're involved with. You might decide to display some of the artwork you made for a practicum in a campus coffee shop where you like to do your homework. Or you might show off what you've learned in your astronomy class by organizing a midnight star-gazing party for your fraternity or sorority. Don't sell yourself short by thinking your outside-of-class activities aren't part of your college experience. The connections between what you're learning and doing in class circle back to your social life, and vice versa.

Using Your Social Groups to Improve Your Grades

Your social circles can even help you do better in your classes. You might have a friend skilled at proofreading who is willing to look over your final research paper in exchange for a nice cup of coffee. You might know someone who is willing to tutor you in a class you're struggling with, or who is willing to work with you on a difficult but important group project.

A group of friends in college is also a great knowledge base. Everyone has different interests, strengths, and skills. Use your social network when and how you can to complement everyone's academic requirements. There's no reason to keep your chemistry skills to yourself when you see a friend struggling in class. Providing and receiving academic help from people in your social circles can help reduce everyone's stress while also letting people receive support from the people they enjoy and respect the most.

Solution #5: Don't Feel the Need to Be Involved with Everything

Even the smallest campuses offer an incredible number of activities. Your social choices during college often revolve around having to choose which things to become involved with rather than struggling to find something in the first place. With seemingly endless choices of social activities and just plain fun things going on, it can be all too easy to find yourself overcommitted, overinvolved, and seriously stressed-out.

During your time in high school, you may have been involved in a lot of activities, both because you enjoyed them and because you thought your involvement would help you get into a good college. And you were likely right on that latter point. Now that you're finally in college, however, how do you choose what you want to be involved in?

Since you have so much freedom when it comes to your social life, try to enjoy it. Don't continue an activity in college simply because you did it in high school—unless you want to. Realizing that you only have to do what you want, when you want, socially, is a major epiphany that many students have while in school. Having that realization, of course, can be difficult, as it often involves letting go of a need to constantly move, to constantly be involved, and to constantly be busy. But once you let yourself relax and just enjoy your social life for what it is, your stress level might unexpectedly shrink—and drastically so.

It can be tempting to want to try everything all at once, especially when you first arrive on campus. There are so many interesting-sounding clubs and events and organizations and activities and programs and traditions. Who wouldn't want to sign up for and be involved in everything?! The reality is, however, that you have a lot of time to do everything you want. Even if you're in an accelerated program, you'll still have several years to spend at your institution. Trying to cram everything in all at once (and all at the beginning) is only going to make you feel stressed-out within a matter of weeks, if not days. You'll feel pulled in a million different directions when, after all, you only have a limited amount of hours in your day, most of which will likely be taken up with the basics of college life: studying, going to class, and taking care of your physical self.

If you can't shake your desire to be involved in a multitude of activities, just do your best to make smart choices about what your involvement looks like. You don't need to assume a leadership role in every club or organization. You don't even have to attend every meeting. Give yourself permission to miss out on every event or social function for certain clubs and organizations, as long as you go to some events and social functions throughout the year. It's okay to just be an occasional participant, just like it's okay to be involved in only one or two things. It's whatever works best for you as an individual and for you as a student. Making sure to keep your social life fun and enjoyable instead of stressful is the ultimate goal.

Solution #6: Learn to Say No

One of the biggest challenges of managing your social life in college is learning how to say no. You will constantly be asked to do things, and you simply won't be able to say yes to everything. Unfortunately, however, it can be too easy to say maybe when you know you should say no—and then find yourself overcommitted and feeling obligated to too many people and situations.

Saying No Doesn't Mean You're Mean

Rest assured that politely saying no doesn't make you mean or flaky or rude. Saying no actually makes you the opposite of all of these things. If you say yes and then don't follow through, your yes answer makes you more rude or flaky than just saying no in the first place.

Because there's so much going on, it's not disrespectful to say no when people ask you to go somewhere, contribute to something, join a club, or help with an upcoming project. No one can do everything all of the time—including you. You'll have to learn how to feel confident and comfortable saying no when you feel like you should say yes, when you feel like you want to say yes, and when people are expecting you to say yes.

It might be awkward and uncomfortable to turn down an invitation or a request for help from a friend. Try to consider what would happen, however, if you said yes to everything. Your academics would suffer, your time management would suffer, and your physical health would suffer. So while it might seem stressful to decline offers left and right, saying no is actually a great stress *reducer*. It gives you the freedom to prioritize as you see fit, to not overwhelm yourself, and to make sure that what you take on is, in fact, what you *want* to take on.

Think of How You'd Advise a Friend

If you're struggling with saying no to others, try to step outside of the situation for a minute. What would you advise a friend to do in your situation? Would you tell her to commit herself to things she didn't have time for or was otherwise not interested in? Would you tell her to keep obliging the requests of others, even if doing so was taking a toll on other areas of her life—including her stress? Of course you wouldn't.

Many people struggle with saying no because they don't want to let down others, they want to be the kind of person who helps out, and they want to be known as someone who is up for some fun. But saying no can actually be the best way to support those around you as well as yourself. After all, if you saw a friend who was overinvolved and having a problem setting boundaries with his or her commitments, you'd most likely think it was smart for him or her to finally start saying no. You'd view it as a sign of strength, organization, and wisdom, not one of disappointment or laziness. Think, too, of the college seniors you admire. They likely are very good at being committed to a limited number of external obligations. They balance what they want to do with what they reasonably can do, and they don't let anyone down—including themselves—by maintain this equilibrium.

Don't Worry about Missing Out

Saying no might make you feel like you're missing out on things everyone else seems to be doing—even if what others are doing doesn't involve the smartest or safest choices. Dr. Lee Mintz, Director of the Center for Student Rights and Responsibilities at San Diego State University, frequently sees students struggling with saying no in a social context. They might be worried about letting people down or are simply agreeing to go along with others because they feel lonely and homesick.

Consequently, Lee observes students who "are willing to do almost anything that their peers are doing in order to feel part of the group and thus lessen the feelings of loneliness." This attempt at connection, she notes, can unfortunately "get many students off to a rocky start with the university—both in terms of policy and in terms of not finding the group that truly matches their interests."

Mintz has come up with a smart tip for students to be able to say no in a way that works for them. She encourages her students to say no and use the line "I can't get in trouble again"—even if it's not true. Having a line like this prepared in advance can help you get out of, or even prevent, a situation you know isn't right for you. Mintz wisely notes that students should say no "not just to avoid getting in trouble with the university, but to avoid wasting time by trying to fit in with people who are not a good fit."

Solution #7: Learn How to Switch Social Cliques

Think back to the person you were when you first started high school. What were you interested in? What were you like? How would you describe yourself? What did you do with your friends for fun? Whom did you hang out with?

Now think of the person you were when you graduated from high school. How did your interests change? How did your friends change? What things did you experience that made a difference in your life? What activities or habits did you grow out of? What activities or habits did you grow into? How would you describe your post-high-school self when compared to your pre-high-school self?

The social and personal growth you go through during your time in college can be equally drastic—if not more so. Your time in college is focused on helping you learn and grow and develop in new ways that you might not even have expected. You learn new things in your classes, see new things in your cocurricular involvement, and meet new people in your social activities. And all of these encounters help you grow as a person, just like you did between your first day of high school and your last.

Because college can be such a growth-intensive period, it's completely normal, if not downright healthy, to make some serious social changes during your college years. The friends you had when you first arrived on campus may not have anything to do with your college life during your junior or senior year. The clubs you joined, events you attended, and places you lived might be drastically different from one year to the next. It's okay. These kinds of changes are all part of the college experience.

Given all that happens during your time in school, let yourself be open to when and how your social life might change. After all, things would be pretty weird if everyone had to stick with the people and activities they connected with during their first few weeks in college.

Organic Changes

A college campus is constantly in a state of change. New students are arriving, people are graduating, people are heading off to study abroad, people are coming back from studying abroad. Some people are moving off campus, some are moving back on campus. Some are transferring in; others are transferring out. There is a constant ebb and flow of new people and ideas, and your social scene should be flexible enough to adapt to this kind of environment.

Sometimes, major changes to your social life and social involvement happen all on their own. You might naturally gravitate to a certain group of folks and leave others behind. Or you might decide to join a formal social group, like a themed residence hall or a fraternity or sorority, which then becomes your primary social scene.

When You Need to Make Proactive Changes

Other times, you might be more interested in making a deliberate effort to change your social scene. Perhaps your friends aren't as supportive of your academics as you'd like. Perhaps your interests have changed and you're looking to expand yourself in other ways. Or perhaps you simply want to branch out and meet new people, try new things, and have new experiences.

If you want to switch from one social group to another, the natural dynamics of college actually make this process pretty easy. Once you decide to gradually transition away from a group of friends, there are likely plenty of other communities that are willing to take you in. If you want to begin that transition, you can:

- Consciously make small and simple changes, like hanging out with new people once or twice a week or going to an occasional event with a new large group.
- Tone down your role in your current social circle; if you're always the organizer or designated driver, for example, try stepping aside one week and see what happens. You'll likely experience a bit of pressure, but everyone should be fine without you. If your current social circles are making you feel stressed over branching out, then that can act as a great reminder of why you're looking for something new in the first place.
- Try out changes in the short-term. Let a club or group of people know that you really need to cut down on your social commitments and focus on your academics this month. Give yourself a month or

so to get used to these changes, and then see how you feel. Do you miss the people you stopped hanging out with, or are you glad to be free from the stress they might have been causing you? Are you relieved to be without so many obligations, or are you looking forward to being involved again?

Ideally, your social experiences in college will help you learn and grow. Sometimes, you might need to make changes to stoke the fire of this growth. Other times, you might just need a break from your usual commitments and routine. The important part to remember, however, is that your college social life should support you and who you are. When you think about how and with whom you spend your social time, you hopefully will think of positive, fun, and even ridiculous memories. You owe it to yourself to prevent stressful, stress-inducing, stress-mongering people and commitments from monopolizing your already precious social time.

Social Stress: Conclusion and Highlights

The social scene in college presents an interesting and difficult conundrum: The very things that allow you to reduce your stress—your cocurricular involvement, friends, and social life—are the same things that can contribute to your stress. Consequently, it can take some mindful attention and wise decision-making to keep things fun and enjoyable when it comes to your college social experience.

- **Invest some time in seeing what's available.** Figuring out your campus social scene can be difficult, but spending a little time learning the who, what, when, where, why, and how can allow you to make informed, healthy choices about your college social life.

Knowing what's available in advance can help ensure that you make the choices that are best for you.

- **Find social groups with expectations and habits that match your own.** Don't feel pressured to engage in certain social activities or behaviors because you think that's what you're supposed to do; engage in activities and behaviors that match your own interests and preferences. Staying true to who you are and what you enjoy is important for avoiding unnecessary social stress during your time in college.

- **Ideally, your friends, activities, and involvement will grow and change—just like you will as a person.** Enjoy the natural social growth and transitions that college involves instead of feeling stressed over them—or, worse, feeling stressed and obligated to keep things how they've always been.

- **Don't let your social life detract from your academics and goal of graduating.** Given your life and priorities as a student, your social situation should complement and even enhance your academic obligations.

- **Know that it's impossible to be involved in everything you might want or feel the need to do.** There simply aren't enough hours in the day to pursue every interesting thing you see in college. You have several years to try new things during your time as a student, so don't stress yourself out by trying to cram everything in all at once.

- **Feel confident, comfortable, and completely justified in saying no.** After all, if you said yes to every opportunity and invitation that came your way, you'd never be able to meet your commitments. Saying no makes you someone who respects your own limitations, who respects the requests of others even as you decline them, and who understands that setting boundaries is a great way to manage and reduce college stress.

- **Be open to the organic shifts and changes that will happen to your social life during your time in school.** Changing social circles, friends, and your cocurricular commitments are all part of your growth experience and, in many ways, part of your education. Rest assured that you can also be proactive about making these changes if you feel that doing so will lead to a more fun, positive, and healthy social experience. Your social life will ideally let you learn, explore, and experience as much as your academics will—yet perhaps while having a lot more fun and with a lot less stress.

CHAPTER 6

Emotional Stress

While you may assume that the most challenging aspects of college involve your brain, it's important to recognize that college can challenge your heart, too. Even those who pride themselves on being emotionally strong can find themselves facing emotional situations—and, consequently, emotional stress—in college.

When you are experiencing emotional stress, everything else in your college life will feel the repercussions. You might find yourself distracted in class, impatient with friends, and emotionally unavailable to those with whom you are usually the closest. One of the more challenging facets of emotional stress is the fact that it can be difficult to recognize, even in yourself. Additionally, it can be difficult to pinpoint exactly what is causing you to be emotionally stressed-out and even more difficult to figure out how to make things better.

Emotional Stress: Identifying the Sources

While it can be a challenge to diagnose yourself as emotionally stressed-out, you likely are pretty well versed in being able to diagnose your symptoms. No matter what your life before college was like, it's practically guaranteed that you experienced some kind of emotional stress. Family problems, drama with friends, relationship ups and downs—these are all part of life, of course, but they can also be major sources of stress. When it comes to your college life, then, it's important to break down your emotional stress to see what areas might need the most attention at any given point in time.

Emotional Stress: The Five Questions

1. *What is my usual emotional state?* How would you describe yourself when you look at your emotional state of health? Are you overall an optimistic person? A pessimistic person? Have you changed recently? How would friends describe you when it comes to your emotions and your emotional state of being? Are you pretty stable when it comes to moods, or do you tend to vacillate depending on the circumstances? What was your normal emotional state during your time in high school? If you have yet to start college, what do you expect your normal emotional state to be in college? If you are already in college, what has your emotional state been like so far?

2. *What are the influences in my life that help me feel happy?* What people help improve your mood, boost your self-confidence, reach your goals, conquer your challenges, and overall become a better you? What activities help you process out stress and feel satisfied and happy? What other resources do you have in your life that contribute to your emotional happiness? What kinds of things do you find help alleviate your emotional stress? What people, activities, habits, or other resources would you like to maintain because of the positive influence they have over you and your emotional well-being? How do you know when you are in a positive, healthy place emotionally?

3. *What are the influences in my life that make me feel unhappy?* What are the main triggers for you to feel unhappy? What

people, places, experiences, or activities add more stress to your life than release? What kinds of things do you often want to avoid doing because of how you feel afterward? What relationships in your life contribute to your emotional stress? What parts of your life would you feel relieved about if they disappeared or faded away? What parts of your life are permanent but causing you emotional stress?

4. *What are the signs that I'm emotionally stressed-out?* How do you know when you are emotionally at your max? Do you recognize the signs yourself by how you are feeling? Do you recognize the signs yourself by how you are acting? Do you need a close friend or family member to provide perspective? Do you feel a slow burn coming, or do you just suddenly and unexpectedly explode? What happens when you feel that you are at your limit emotionally? What signs do you give yourself? What signs do you give others?

5. *How do I usually deal with emotional stress?* When you find yourself dealing with an emotional situation, what's your initial reaction? What's your short-term reaction? What's your long-term reaction? Do you react differently depending on the people and context, or is your reaction more standard regardless of the circumstances? Are you trying to change how you deal with emotional stress? What resources do you tap into? What resources do you pull away from? How do you get yourself from being completely emotionally stressed-out to a more healthy, balanced emotional state?

Finding Solutions

Fortunately, there is a wide range of resources available to help you deal with emotional stress during your time in college. From the campus counseling center to your own, internal strengths, there are definitely ways to find support. The first step is learning to understand where exactly your emotional stress is coming from. Once you know that, you can find the most effective solution.

Solution #1: Set Realistic Expectations

One of the biggest emotional challenges you are likely to face in college is setting realistic expectations. Your family will have expectations about your course of study; your professors will have expectations about your academic performance. And when it comes to your emotions, it's likely you'll have some expectations—whether consciously or not—about what your college experience will be like.

It's important to note, however, that college is much different from high school, especially as it relates to your emotional stress levels. Just like your new academic life, your college emotional life is going to be a new experience. The stakes are higher, which means that you're more likely to emotionally invest in things that you might have brushed off several years ago. You also are transitioning from being a younger, less educated person to a college-educated adult. With these changes, of course, comes a wide range of emotions. And any kind of emotional change is likely to cause some emotional stress, too.

Think of Entering College Like Moving to a New Country

In some ways, the experience of going to college can cause what might seem like culture shock. Shirley O'Neil, MEd, LPC, and a certified school counselor, notes that, "Going to college is like going to a new country. You need time to adjust and see what you like/don't like, whom you want to be friends with, what it is going to take to succeed in classes, what activities are fun, how you want to manage your time, and even how you want to redefine yourself." You would most likely be patient with yourself and expect some emotional adjustment if you were, as O'Neil notes in her analogy, heading off to a new country.

Setting realistic expectations for your adjustment to and experience in college requires similar patience. "College is a big change and putting pressure on oneself to get certain grades or attain certain athletic goals is a recipe for anxiety…Once the student has figured out what their college is like, then they can create expectations for themselves. Expectations are unrealistic if they cause anxiety."

Although things can be coming at you during your time in school at a seemingly rapid pace, be patient with yourself. You are learning and growing and experiencing all kinds of new things. You are learning to question and analyze and think critically—and not just in the classroom. With this kind of growth and curiosity come growing pains.

This major, and often steep, learning curve is part of the process of being in school. Many people, when thinking about college life in general, don't consider the emotional side of what it's like as a college student. Because of this, you might feel like your emotional stress and struggles are a sign that you aren't doing well, that you are emotionally weak, or that you just need to suck it up and get with the program.

Experiencing Some Stress Is Normal

While adapting is important, experiencing some emotional stress during your time in school is actually a good sign. It means you are challenging yourself, facing conflict and struggles, taking risks, and

168 College Stress Solutions

exploring. Failure and struggle—whether it's in your classes, with your finances, or even with your emotions—is part of the journey. Your emotional investment, after all, indicates that you are valuing your education. You are dedicating a lot of time and intellectual effort to earning your degree. You are also investing quite a bit financially in your education. It's absolutely normal, and even quite good, for you to be emotionally invested in your experience, too.

Go Easy on Yourself

Setting an expectation that you'll be able to handle everything, emotionally speaking, that comes your way is unrealistic. Things will be hard; it would be impossible to turn off your emotional response to life's ups and downs if you weren't in school, so why should you expect yourself to be able to do so when you are in school? While you can expect yourself to make it through your low points and come out with your chin up, you can't expect yourself never to struggle. Let yourself experience the emotional speed bumps that college presents without being too hard on yourself for it.

Instead of expecting yourself to not feel emotionally vulnerable, to not have emotional challenges, and to be emotionally stoic during your time in school, expect to experience some emotional stress along the way. This more realistic expectation can help you deal more positively with whatever comes your way, and ideally can help reduce your stress as a result.

Solution #2: Manage Homesickness

An almost universal challenge among college students who are far from home—especially in their first semester—is homesickness. Interestingly, even if no one you know on your campus is talking about being homesick, they undoubtedly are feeling it. It's a huge part of students' experience, even if no one feels comfortable admitting it.

You are, after all, likely in an entirely new environment. The people, places, routines, culture, and traditions are all new. And since a feeling of home and comfort comes from a feeling of familiarity, it's no wonder that—since nothing feels familiar—you're yearning for a sense of belonging.

College homesickness can definitely be a major emotional stressor. It can be hard to get out of your room and go to class, participate in activities, and feel at ease in your new "home" when all you're longing for is your old one. It can be all too easy to head home for the weekends, where you can enjoy your familiar (and much more comfy) bed, indulge in home cooking, and overall feel at ease.

Unfortunately, the very things that tend to alleviate homesickness only do so over the short-term. Over the long-term, heading home too often or staying in your residence hall room actually makes homesickness worse. Sometimes, even your best attempts to make your homesickness go away only end up adding to it—and your stress levels.

The best way to approach homesickness, then, is to take a deep breath and summon up your courage. Try the following five strategies and see what works best:

1. **Remind yourself why you went to college in the first place.** It was to expand your horizons, improve your job and career opportunities, and maybe even make a difference in the world. It was to empower yourself and others to make positive changes, and to ensure that you could provide down the road for yourself and those you love. In essence, you went to college to learn new things, meet new people, experience new

challenges, and grow as a person. And of course doing so is going to be difficult, especially at first! Don't sell yourself short or break the promise you made to yourself to step outside your comfort zone. Growing as a person is emotionally hard because it involves struggle. And that struggle often makes you crave home and familiarity.

2. **Only go home once over the next eight weeks.** That's it. Yes, really. It can be hard, and if your family is close, it can be even harder. But going home prevents you from building connections, finding a sense of community, and establishing a new sense of home at your school. Sure, it will be uncomfortable and even lonely at times. But there's just no way to adjust to your new college life if you're not physically present in it. Use the emotions that are pulling you home to pull you out of your comfort zone and into your new life instead.

3. **Only let your family visit once over the next twelve weeks.** That's it. Yes, really. Having your parents, other family members, or even significant other from back home come to visit you can indeed help. But these kinds of visits can also do more harm than good in the same way that visits home can—they prevent you from venturing out and forming new relationships. After all, if your parents are in town, are you more likely to head to a club meeting and grab dinner with your quadmates, or are you more likely to go to Target and dinner afterward with your family? Give yourself a chance to form new connections on campus. By doing so, you can alleviate the emotional stress that you're feeling from being homesick; you can also form friendships, relationships, and other connections

that will help you handle the emotional stress you might encounter later on in your college experience.

4. **Don't call people back home more than once or twice a week.** Talking daily on the phone with your mom, twice daily on Skype with your partner, or texting all day, every day, with your best friend back home might make you feel better for a short time. But when the conversation is over, you're still stuck right where you started: college. And you likely missed out on some great opportunities to attend an event, listen to a speaker, meet new people, and get involved in an interesting club or organization. Sometimes, too, talking too much with people back home will actually make you feel more homesick and emotionally distressed. Plan instead to talk to your parents on Tuesday nights, so you can spend other nights attending social events, doing your reading, and otherwise participating in your college life. It is those kinds of experiences that are going to help conquer your homesickness, not frequent calls and chats with people back home.

5. **Request care packages.** Visits home, visits from family, and frequent communication with the people you miss the most can often backfire on your attempts to deal with your homesickness. Care packages, however, are another story. They can make you feel loved and appreciated, can be a wonderful surprise that snaps you out of an emotional funk, and, of course, can provide you with a bunch of tasty treats. Don't be too proud to ask your friends and family for care packages! They can be great pick-me-ups when you need a virtual hug from back home. Your parents can bake your favorite baked goods and send them along, buy your favorite snacks from the store,

or even use an online company that specifically makes care packages for college students. They can also send pictures and other mementos that remind you of home—and that can help make your room or apartment feel more like home. Regardless of what they contain, care packages can be a great resource to help you finally get the upper hand on your homesickness and the emotional stress it causes.

Solution #3: Try to Find a Community That's Right for You

Let's say you muster up your courage, quash down your homesickness, grab your keys, and head out of your room in an attempt to connect with your college community and all that it offers. So…just where should you go, exactly? What should you try to do?

It can be all too easy to become overwhelmed with choices in college while simultaneously feeling like there's nothing that suits you. Emotionally, that might make you feel very stuck. There are tons of things happening on your campus, and everyone seems incredibly busy, but you aren't sure where to go or how everything works. In essence, you aren't sure where you fit in.

Be Brave and Try *Something*

The best approach to take—whether you're just starting college, just starting at a new college after transferring, or even just starting a new semester—is to simply be brave and try something. What do you like to do in your spare time? What kinds of things interest you on a personal, intellectual, political, spiritual, or community level? What makes you feel satisfied at the end of the day: Volunteering? Having political debates? Attending a worship service? Being around music and art? Start with what resonates with you on a personal level and go from there. Even if you start with something that doesn't quite seem right, you can at least connect with people who have similar interests—and with whom you can start a conversation.

The only "wrong" way to be involved in college is to have your involvement be a detriment to your health or your academics (or those of others, of course). There's no such thing as making a social mistake or joining the wrong club. If you attend a meeting or two of a certain club and decide it's not for you, it's no big deal. The people won't hate you. You won't be considered a dork. And if the people in the club do hate you and consider you a dork, it's probably good you left them behind anyway.

People move in all kinds of circles in school. New students come into communities like clubs, residence halls, fraternities and sororities, and religious groups all of the time. Part of college is exploring new ideas, which includes finding the things that aren't quite right.

Be Patient

With that in mind, it's important to be patient with yourself when it comes to finding the right community at your school and really finding a place for you to fit in. It takes a lot of time, a lot of effort, and a lot of patience, which of course can be emotionally stressful. It takes time for friendships to grow, just like it takes time for you to decide that you really enjoy attending a certain club's weekly meetings—or not.

Changes Are Okay

The things (and even people) that made you feel completely connected and at home during your first year of college might not provide that same sense of connection in your junior year. This doesn't mean that anything is wrong, that you made a mistake, or that you need to work harder to re-establish those connections. It simply means that you are growing as a person, and part of that growth involves branching out as you get older and spend more time in school.

Instead of viewing these kinds of social changes as emotionally stressful, try to look at them as a positive in your life. By taking time to find the right friendships and truly connect with the right social circles, you are, in fact, being emotionally wise instead of inept. By deciding to branch out from your usual communities in an effort to find ones that better support the person you are becoming, you are not being emotionally shallow; you are adding emotional depth to your life by challenging yourself and exploring the resources available to you.

In essence, the ways you connect—or don't connect—during your time in school are going to change. Sometimes you'll feel completely at home; sometimes you'll feel completely lost. And both are okay. Most of the time, you'll likely feel somewhere in the middle. Rest assured that fitting in and finding a community at your school is an ongoing, intense process that is likely to be emotionally challenging at times. The key, however, is making sure that you note the difference between emotionally challenging and emotionally stressful.

Solution #4: Use Your Religion as a Resource

For some students, religion can provide an excellent bridge between their time before, during, and after college. If you have been or are thinking of becoming religiously active, college can be a great time to confirm your faith or even help you explore other faiths that you might not have previously considered.

Religious communities are a great place to connect with people who share your beliefs and values. The familiarity that comes with traditions, cultures, and rites associated with many religions can help you conquer homesickness, feel connected to your new community, and simply relax and have fun. You can find an emotional connection with people in a religious club, in a practicing religious group, or even in a religious organization located near your campus. Religion can be a great way for you to alleviate some emotional stress while helping you feel rested, restored, and revitalized.

Alyson Solomon, a rabbi in Los Angeles, believes that a religious community can help meet the unique needs of students during their time in school. "Particularly in college, students yearn for a sense of home and belonging," she notes. "We want to be seen, supported, loved, and nurtured. A religious or spiritual community can be such a place for spiritual seekers and young people looking for meaning, guidance, support, substance, and sustenance." Connecting with people and having a shared experience together can, in fact, do wonders for your stress levels in all kinds of ways. "Dance class might be a great place to sweat and fraternity parties might be fun," Solomon says, "but a spiritual home has the potential to nourish the mind, body, and spirit."

The religious leaders on campus—whether they're fellow students, graduate students, club advisers, or formal religious figures—can also help you during your time in school. Connecting with them and seeking their mentorship and advice can be a great way to gain perspective and a sense of home. College can be incredibly challenging in all kinds of ways, so let your faith be both your guide and a source of strength.

Religion Can Help Homesickness

A religious community can also help provide a sense of home when you need it most. If you miss going to weekly services, see what's available on your campus. If holidays or other cultural events are coming up, see what's being planned. Better yet, see how you can be involved in the planning. If you need a place to pray, meditate, or simply find some solace, see what's offered for students like you. Even if there isn't a formal building available for worship, there might be classrooms or certain meeting rooms that are being made available for members of your faith.

A religious community can be an excellent resource in helping you process out your emotional stress. It can also be a great way for you to prevent emotional stress in the first place. Even seemingly simple activities, like hanging out for a few hours on the weekend with people who share your beliefs, can do wonders in helping you refocus and reprioritize. And with that reorientation often comes a renewed strength and ability to keep your stress—especially your emotional stress—in perspective.

Solution #5: Try Meditation

Although it may sound counterintuitive at first, finding time to let your mind rest during your time in school is incredibly important when it comes to managing stress. Your brain is actively engaged from the moment you wake up until the moment you go to sleep. You're constantly thinking about what to do next, where to go next, what's expected of you next. With that constant whirring, however, comes a need to simply let your brain relax.

This is, of course, easier said than done. As any college student can tell you, there are very few locations on campus that can help facilitate a mental pause. Even at 2:00 in the morning, the residence halls, coffee shops, and labs are full of busy people. Unfortunately, this constant whirlwind of activity only further exacerbates the need for self-reflection and meditation. Meditating, even for a short period of time each week, can help calm the chaos that leads to stress—and yet finding the actual space to take a break and meditate can be quite a challenge in and of itself.

You just might be surprised at what you'll learn—and how your stress will decrease—if you take a few minutes to mix up your schedule and make an appointment someplace quiet with yourself. Even if you've never formally meditated before, making the time to just sit and reflect can quickly turn into one of your most effective stress busters.

Keep in mind that meditation doesn't have to be a long, exhaustive process. Simply spending five or ten minutes with yourself can have a significant impact on your stress levels and on your ability to concentrate. In fact, the days when you feel like you couldn't possibly spare five minutes to stop and meditate might just be the days when you most need to do so.

Where to Meditate

So just where can you go when you really, truly need a quite space to sit and think?

A Carrel in the Library

While most people think of libraries as quiet places, the college library can quickly turn into a social place if you're not smart about what you do once you show your student ID and pass through the doors. You may have the best of intentions when you come in, find a table, set up your laptop, and start getting to work. But then your sorority sister whom you haven't seen in a while walks by and wants to catch up, your softball teammate has an update on the game this weekend, and your suitemate sees you and decides to set up his stuff, too. Before you know it, your quiet plans have suddenly turned into a not-so-quiet group activity.

Reserving or renting a carrel may seem antisocial, but it's a great way to enjoy a little nook of your own. You don't have to talk with anyone, and the closed door or barrier indicates to others that you are busy and don't want to be disturbed. Consider spending thirty minutes a week in your carrel, not doing anything but meditating and reflecting on the past seven days. Make an appointment with yourself by marking it down in your calendar. Transform the physical space into a mental space, too, that allows you to rest and reflect in the calm and quiet.

Find a Big, Empty Space

You know those big event spaces, rooms, and lecture halls that usually hold hundreds (if not thousands) of people? Guess what happens to them when they're not in use? They just sit there, waiting for students to come along for the next big event.

If you need a quiet place to meditate and take some time "away," peek into one of the larger spaces on campus. You can sneak into a chair and enjoy your own sacred space with no one else around. This can be a great location to reflect on your college experience so far or even just to tune out and get a few quiet moments to yourself.

Additionally, if you're stressed-out and needing motivation, consider heading to the large campus venue where your graduation will take place. You can focus on what graduation day will look like, how amazing it will feel to toss your cap with your classmates, and what you need to do to get from here to there. Meditating can often help you regain some perspective and motivation, and finding a large venue that celebrates the best that your college has to offer can be a great place to help facilitate that thought process.

✪ Straight from a Student: Meditation and Visualization

Ryinta Brown, a senior at the University of Michigan-Dearborn, finds focusing on the future to be an excellent motivator and stress reducer. When things become stressful, one of Brown's most effective techniques is to contextualize what is happening within the larger picture. In essence, she imagines her own graduation. "Picture yourself on stage shaking the dean of your college's hand and receiving your diploma," she suggests. "I found that my stress level almost disappeared when I stopped looking at where I was, but looked at where I was going."

Visit an Athletic Venue

Think like an athlete. Just like the larger campus venues, athletic facilities are often quiet, neglected places when they're not hosting major events. Consequently, if you need to find a simple, easy-to-access location for a few minutes of meditation time, think creatively about spaces that often host sporting events.

One added benefit of sneaking away to, say, the softball fields is that you can end up getting some quiet time outside. The sunshine, fresh air, and sounds of nature can do wonders for your stress levels. Mix in twenty minutes of meditation, where you simply let your thoughts come and go as they please, and you have a great recipe for a quick stress reducer.

Where to Start

If you're unsure of what athletic locations are available, download a campus map and take a look at the different sport fields and stadiums that are listed. If you played lacrosse, soccer, softball, basketball, rugby, beach volleyball, or any other sport, where would you head for practice or a game?

If you're still unsure of where to go, think like a spectator. Where on campus could you go to watch an athletic event? Any quiet place that has chairs, bleachers, or a large grassy area can quickly become your next meditation spot. After you've spent a few minutes doing some deep breathing and meditating, you can leave your stress on the field and head back to your usual college activities.

Solution #6: Challenge Yourself to Step Outside of Your Comfort Zone

One of the biggest challenges—especially emotionally—of being in college is the constant assault on your comfort zone. You might be put in a living situation with people you aren't sure you like, you might be asked to research and discuss something in class that you don't fully understand, and you might be exposed to new ideas and activities that definitely aren't what you're used to.

All of these new, unfamiliar, and even uncomfortable situations require that you step outside of your comfort zone if you are to truly learn from and engage with them. Unfortunately, making this brave step is easier said than done.

After all, who wants to feel awkward and uneasy all of the time? Being challenged is good, but not when it starts to stress you out. It's perfectly reasonable to want to avoid situations that put you in an unfamiliar emotional space, especially when you already have too many demands on yourself from other areas of your college life.

You likely went to college, however, to learn new things and have new experiences. And while this process will be enjoyable, it can also be uncomfortable. In fact, it *should* be uncomfortable from time to time. It would be a shame to graduate, look back at your time in school, and say to yourself, "I wish I would have branched out a little..."

It can be downright nerve-racking to think about trying certain activities, doing certain events, or taking certain risks. Perhaps you've never been involved in any kind of leadership but are thinking of running for vice president of your club. Perhaps you absolutely hate being in front of crowds but really want to join a fraternity or sorority. Perhaps you've always been quiet in class but want to join a small discussion group your favorite professor is leading.

All of these actions involve stepping outside of your comfort zone, and that can be scary. It can even be stressful, albeit in a good way. But not taking risks and challenging yourself should be scarier than trying something new or possibly making a mistake.

In a sense, your entire college experience is like a ropes course. You signed up for the challenge. You prepared yourself, you have safety gear on, you're with a group of people whom you may or may not know but that you're stuck with. Some of the challenges in front of you look ridiculously easy, while others seem downright impossible. And what appears terrifying to you might seem simple to someone else. Your overall experience in school comprises each of the elements. If you don't go through the course, your overall experience will be lacking in many ways. Challenge yourself to make it through the elements that present the biggest challenges for you, as these might end up being your biggest accomplishments. But you won't know unless you try.

In essence, don't let your biggest regret of college be that you have no regrets. Not failing in something you cared about—and ended up regretting later—means you never challenged yourself in a way where failure was an option. And while trying new things can be emotionally stressful, the rewards from doing so can also be incredibly emotionally rewarding.

Solution #7: Consider Transferring

Some students are simply unhappy at their college or university. Before you make any drastic changes, it's important to examine what it means if you "just don't like it" at your school. There are lots of ways to not like your college experience, but not all of them warrant transferring to another institution—or, more significantly, dropping out altogether.

Why Transfer?

There are very legitimate reasons to transfer, such as:

* Financially, you might need to transfer to an institution that is lower in cost or that is closer to home.
* Personally, you might need to transfer to an institution that is able to offer you better support services or that allows you to be more readily available to deal with personal obligations.
* Academically, you might need to transfer to an institution that offers a program, major, or degree that better aligns with your interests and goals.
* Socially, you might need to transfer to an institution where the student body is more of a match for your personality.

You likely have a school mismatch in more than one area if you are thinking of transferring. This mismatch can cause all kinds of stress—especially emotional stress, as feeling like you aren't in the right place (and are actively in the wrong place) can be emotionally difficult.

Do Some Soul-Searching

If you're thinking of transferring, you owe it to yourself to do some serious and deep thinking about the decision. Just like choosing to apply to and attend college is a major life choice, choosing to change that choice is a significant process that warrants significant reflection. Consider walking yourself through the following exercises:

1. **Make a list of the things you don't like at your school.** They can be people, places, or experiences. They can be things that have happened or things that aren't happening. They can be academic, financial, emotional, or social in nature. There are no rules for writing down what you don't like. Just write down whatever comes to mind.

2. **Imagine another college.** It can be a specific school that you're thinking of transferring to, or just a general type of institution that comes to mind. Looking at your list, how does this new institution compare? What does it offer that your current institution does not? Does it have different people? Different academic opportunities, like a different major? A different social scene? A different campus culture? Connections to those you miss the most? Different opportunities for what you want to do in your future career?

3. **Make a list of your goals for life after college.** What do you want to do? What kind of job would you like to have? It

doesn't have to be particularly specific, either. It could be that you want a job that pays enough for you to support a family, or that you'd generally like a job doing something in education. Write down anything that comes to mind. You can describe what you want in your financial future, your professional future, or your personal future. There are no right or wrong items to put on this list.

4. **Once you have your lists completed, return to your first list and ask yourself a key question:** Are the things making you unhappy at your current institution things that you can change? If so, look at your other lists. Will a new institution allow you to make those changes? Will it provide those changes automatically—say, because of its physical location or because a major is offered there that your current institution doesn't have? Or will it only provide the possibility for change? Additionally, look at your list of what you'd like for your future. How would transferring have an impact on those goals? Will it get you closer to them? Farther away? Or do your goals need to be revised as well, given your experience at your current institution?

You're Not Alone

Rest assured that transferring colleges does not mean that you made a mistake, that you messed up, or that you've done something wrong. In fact, the National Student Clearinghouse Research Center reported in 2012 that one-third of all students transfer before earning a degree. So if you are thinking of (or even do end up) transferring, you might be a lot more like your peers than you realize.

Make an Informed Choice

Whether transferring is an obvious choice for your situation or just something you're starting to think about, it's important to make sure your decision is a well-informed one.

- Make an appointment to talk with your academic adviser about the reasons you're thinking of transferring. Be sure to do it in person; this is one of those situations that shouldn't be handled over e-mail.
- Talk with your friends on campus and your friends back home.
- Talk with your family.
- Talk with the financial aid office so you are completely clear on what the financial repercussions would be if (and when) you were to transfer.
- Talk to the registrar's office, too, so that you know in advance what will be reflected on your transcript.
- The most important conversation to have, however, is with yourself. Try to think about why you chose college, and your current school, in the first place. Think about what you hoped to learn and experience. Think about what your goals were and what you hoped to accomplish before you graduated. Think about how this might change were you to transfer, and what those changes would look like.

Transferring can indeed be a smart choice for many students, and it's clearly a common choice. And while that information can be comforting, it also has nothing to do with your individual situation. If you have legitimate reasons and a desire to transfer, don't be so harsh on yourself that you end up exacerbating the stress you're already feeling.

Let the process of transferring be a way for you to work through the stress toward a calming, stress-free solution.

Solution #8: Talk Yourself Out of Transferring

While transferring can provide a great resolution for college students in certain situations, it may not always be the best decision for everyone. In fact, in some cases, transferring might only make your college experience more stressful.

Transferring might be an unwise choice for you if going to a new college or university is only going to duplicate the problems you are experiencing at your current institution. For example, if you are not making friends and connecting socially because you are staying in your room too much, how will this change at a new school? Will you still be inclined to let your shy side overcome your desire to meet people? And will you put yourself through considerable effort—and stress—by simply transferring to a new situation that turns out to be nearly identical to the one you're in now?

If you're thinking of transferring, continue to ask yourself difficult, challenging questions about your motivations. What will be different at a new institution? What will be the same? What will you do to emotionally connect and find a sense of community? Why are you not doing those things now, at your current school? What is holding you back from finding solutions to things that you can change right now?

It can be very difficult to make changes and improve your current situation if you're always looking for greener pastures. Going to a new school, however, isn't always the solution; it's simply a new place. It can be difficult to confront your own fears and struggles, but it's also critically important. Have you really tried your best to make it work where you are? Have you given it your all? Are there things you know you should attempt to do, but deep inside you know you haven't given them a legitimate shot?

You worked hard to get where you are. Honor yourself, your commitment, and your hard work by keeping that momentum up, even when things are difficult. Give yourself and your current school every last opportunity to make things work. If it doesn't work out, that's okay. Just be mindful that you don't end up duplicating your problems and frustrations somewhere else, as your emotional stress will make sure to tag along, too.

Solution #9: Seek Counseling on Campus

Sometimes, things simply feel like they're all too much to handle. College is, after all, incredibly challenging. The academic requirements, financial obligations, personal struggles, social scene, emotional challenges, and family expectations all add up. And sometimes they add up to something that feels larger than yourself.

Unfortunately, people sometimes have the (positively silly) idea that there's something wrong with asking for a little help. There's not. You likely would ask your professor for some help with an upcoming assignment or exam you're struggling with. You'd definitely ask the financial aid office for help if you couldn't make ends meet without some assistance. And you probably wouldn't even think twice about stopping into a campus health clinic to get treatment for a bad cold or cough.

Just like your professors, the financial aid office, and the campus health clinic, the college counseling office is part of a larger university system that is there to help you. People struggle while they're in school because it's really, really hard. Struggling is part of the experience. And sometimes, you might want or need some help along the way.

Forget the stigma you might have about people who head to a counseling center. Seeing a counselor can be liberating and empowering. You can pop in for one visit, have weekly visits over a long period of time, attend a support group, or just go once for a screening. There's really no reason why you shouldn't at least see what your campus counseling center has to offer. The counselors there understand what it means to be a student and are particularly trained (and skilled) in helping students deal with whatever comes their way. You can talk to a counselor about time management skills, stress-reduction techniques, or even because you're feeling down in the dumps about a recent breakup. Your family might be becoming too much to handle and you need some skills to deal with them. You might also have experienced a traumatic event and both want and need to connect with a professional to help you work through what happened.

"There are all sorts of bumps along the road of life, and college life is no exception," says Barbara Thomas, PhD, Senior Director of Counseling and Psychological Services at the University of San Francisco. She recommends heading to your campus counseling center for some support if you are experiencing any of the following:

- Changes in eating, sleeping, an ability to focus, social behavior, or grades (in the wrong direction)
- A breakup of a relationship, or of your parents' relationship
- A loss (including the family dog!);
- Drug abuse
- Sexual assault
- Sexual and/or gender identity exploration
- Persistent feelings of anxiety or depression

The stresses that you have to deal with may be unexpected or expected, planned or unplanned—but they can all cause emotional distress. If you at all think that seeing a counselor would be beneficial, call, e-mail, or just pop in to the college counseling center. They are there to help you and can be one of your best resources. Not reaching out and utilizing such a powerful resource is a missed opportunity for you to greatly reduce the stress during your college years—and beyond.

Emotional Stress: Conclusion and Highlights

Being emotionally stressed can be incredibly challenging because this kind of stress in particular can run quite deep. When you are emotionally in turmoil, all other aspects of your college life will feel it and you will struggle with maintaining your holistic sense of well-being. Given the importance of one's emotional stress management, it's critical to know how to find solutions to your emotional stressors—and when to ask for help.

- **Set realistic expectations for yourself.** You might be putting yourself through unnecessary emotional ups and downs because your expectations are too high. College is a completely new and unique experience. It will take time to adjust, and struggling along the way indicates that you are challenging yourself, not failing.
- **Know that it is normal to be homesick.** It's unreasonable to expect that you won't miss the things you have known for so long and take the greatest comfort in. Your job in college, however, is not to forget about home but to build a home away from home. Stay connected with your home base and your support system while also remembering to branch out and connect with your new college community. While homesickness may cause some emotional stress, the best way

to combat it is to find people and places at your school that you can become emotionally connected to.

- **Be patient.** It takes time, effort, patience, and mistakes to fit in and find a community in college. Don't expect things to happen instantly or organically. You will have to go to events, meet people, be brave, take risks, and be patient in order to find out where you best fit in.

- **Religion can be a very powerful, personal resource for you.** You can connect with a religious community, with religious leaders, with traditions and rites, and with people who share your values. A strong religious community and connection can also help alleviate your emotional stress, whether it's through events that provide a sense of comfort and familiarity or through a support network that helps you deal with emotional challenges you encounter.

- **Meditate to keep your emotional stress in check.** Make an appointment with yourself to meditate and reflect at least once a week, if not once a day. Even a few minutes in the morning can do wonders for your emotional health. Find a place on campus that supports the way you like to meditate best and make it part of your routine.

- **Challenge yourself to step outside of your comfort zone.** While doing so may seem emotionally straining, it doesn't have to be emotionally stressful. You should learn and stretch and grow during your college years. Stepping outside of your comfort zone is part of that process, but it requires bravery and initiative. Make it happen!

- **Transferring can be a wise choice if the situation you're transferring to provides resources and opportunities that are not available to you at your current school.** Transferring can be an unwise choice, however, if you are going to go through all the trouble of starting afresh somewhere new only to duplicate your problems. If you are thinking of transferring, just make sure your decision is informed and well thought out. You want to alleviate your emotional stress, not exacerbate it.

- **Utilize the campus counseling center whenever and however you think you need to.** These centers are fantastic resources if you're struggling, regardless of how small or large your issue is. Whether you want to be proactive and get some support about, say, your stress management, or you want to be reactive and get support because of a traumatic event that you've experienced, the college counseling center is your best bet. Don't let social stigmas or stereotypes—from you or others—prevent you from getting the help you need or want.

CHAPTER 7

Family Stress

For some students, ~~family is a source of great strength during their time in school~~. Family members and family dynamics are positive and supportive. Trips home can be restorative, fun, and filled with lots of good people and memories.

For other students, family is a serious source of stress. Unhealthy relationships and behaviors all combine into a lack of support during one's time in school. Long weekends, holiday breaks, and even summers present awkward decisions about whether or not to return home. ~~College can become an escape of sorts~~, even if that escape is tinged with guilt and conflict.

Family can ~~bring a wide and complicated range of dynamics into your college experience~~. Whether your family is the best imaginable or one filled with challenges, your family undoubtedly features heavily in your college life. Additionally, your family may be helpful in some ways and frustrating in others. ~~How you deal with~~ and ~~balance your family~~ during your time in school ~~will have a significant impact~~ on everything from what you study to what you do socially. And, of course, ~~how you deal with your family will~~ ~~have a significant impact on your stress~~—for good or for bad.

Family Stress: Identifying the Sources

Finding the source of your family stress takes a bit of patience. It can be frustrating to deal with family sometimes, and easy to ignore them or brush off their good intentions because you know they will love and support you regardless. At the same time, however, when things are rocky with your family or with your relationship with them, the stress can be significant and unavoidable. Finding and understanding where your family stress is coming from is perhaps the most important step you can take to reducing it—if not preventing it altogether.

Family Stress: The Five Questions

1. *How does my family support my college goals and dreams?* Think about when your family has really helped you through a rough time. What did their support look like? How did they know you needed extra support? How can you make sure to communicate this same need if it arises during your college years? What ways do they support you the best? What specific actions do your family take that enable you to deal with stress and achieve your dreams? How might their support need to change during your time in school?

2. *How does my family distract—if even unintentionally—from my college goals and dreams?* What kinds of things does your family do that add to your stress? What kinds of family issues, relationships, or behaviors immediately make you tense up when you think about your family? What kinds of unhealthy patterns does your family have that you don't want with you in college? What happens when your family is adding to your stress? How does it feel? How can you disconnect from it when that happens?

3. *What are the most supportive and successful methods my family has for dealing with stress?* How does your family, as a unit, handle

stress? What approaches do they use that work well? How can you incorporate these same methods into your college life? What kinds of challenges—for example, financial—does your family handle really well? What has your entire family learned over the past five years, for instance, that better enables everyone, as individuals, to deal with stress? How can you transfer these family skills to situations that arise in college?

4. *Are certain family members exceedingly good—or bad—at helping to reduce my college stress?* How available will they be during your entire time in college? When you think of the members of your family who are good at preventing or dealing with stress, which people come to mind? What do they do well? Are their skills and approaches ones you can try to mimic on your own? Or would you benefit from some direct mentorship? How can you reach out to these people when you need them most? How will you know when it's time to reach out?

5. *What kinds of patterns and behaviors does my family have that I don't want to have as part of my college life?* What kinds of specific situations do you know will be stressful and ones you know you want to avoid altogether? What other major sources of stress might your family add to the other stress that you're feeling in college? How can you identify and avoid those sources? What proactive approaches can you take to distance yourself from these stresses? What reactive approaches can you take to let them fade away if they do start to creep into your college life?

Finding Solutions

Perhaps one of the most challenging factors of dealing with your family in college is the fact that many, if not most, families can simultaneously be stress reducers and stress inducers. While they may do a great job of helping you talk through situations and come up with solutions during phone calls, your family members may drive you nuts by nagging you to call them more frequently. Or, while they have helpful tips about how to sort out and manage your financial aid, their dating advice is definitely something you could do without. Fortunately, there are lots of ways to handle many different scenarios.

Solution #1: Be Honest with Your Family about Performance, Potential, and Possibilities

One of the more challenging aspects of dealing with your family during your time in college is just that: having your entire family involved in an experience that primarily focuses on you.

Even if you feel like you worked your tail off to get yourself into your school, it's a very, very rare student who is able to do so completely on his or her own. It is especially important to acknowledge all that your family has worked for, sacrificed, and dreamed of before you officially enrolled in classes. It's also important to think about all of the things your family has done that you simply were—and maybe still are—unaware of: late-night, college-focused conversations between your parents while you were sleeping, for example, or extra hours at work so that your tuition bills can be paid on time. When a student goes to college, the entire family is involved in one way or another.

Because of this simple fact, and no matter how independent you may feel, you must remember all of those who came before you. Perhaps you're the first in your family to go to college; perhaps you're the sixth generation to go to your particular institution. Regardless, those who walked before you paved the way.

Family history easily transforms into your family's presence during your college years. And with your family's presence comes their expectations. Even if they haven't voiced it, your family undoubtedly has expectations of what you should and can do during your time in school. These kinds of expectations may focus on what you're going to major in, what sports you'll excel at, how you'll be involved socially, or even what you'll do for a career after you graduate. Additionally, siblings or extended family members who went to college before you might have set a precedent. Your own performance and interests in high school may also play a role in your family's college expectations.

Given this pressure-based (and stress-inducing) context, it is critically important to make sure you are clear about what expectations you have that are your own—and what expectations you have that come from external sources. Your family may insist that you major in something "practical," for example, even though your heart is drawn to a major they don't respect. If you come from a long line of people who work in a particular profession (such as teachers, ministers, or doctors), the assumption might be that you'll continue in this line of work as well.

If you have the same expectations of yourself that your family does, that's great. If not, be mindful of the difference. What do you think is reasonable to expect of yourself regarding your academic performance, for instance? What kinds of things are you interested in doing socially? What would you like to be involved with cocurricularly? Would you still be interested in these things if your family were out of the picture? If so, why? What kinds of motivators do you have behind your own college expectations? In essence: What are you working toward and striving for that is a dream of your own making, and what are you working toward and striving for that is someone else's expectation?

Not being clear on the difference between your own and someone else's expectations can be a major source of family stress. You might dread phone calls with your parents, for example, because they want to ask how you are doing in certain classes—and you are trying to avoid the fact that you don't like those classes and are thinking of switching majors. Or you might be participating in Rush Week for a certain fraternity your father and grandfather were also in, even though you can't stand the students who now make up the fraternity membership.

Things can become stressful quickly when it comes to managing your family's expectations. The key comes in knowing the difference between what's motivating you internally, and what you're feeling pressured to achieve or accomplish for the sake of others.

What Are Your Family's Expectations?

Once you're able to identify your family's expectations, you can work toward making them non-stress-inducing factors in your college life.

A good general attitude to take when dealing with family pressures, family expectations, and, consequently, family stress is to try to keep things in perspective. Dr. Linda L. Thomas Worthy, Educational Consultant and Student Development Specialist, says, "For many family members, their expectation for the student's success is based on their own experiences and desires to see the student do better...or to beat the odds." In other words, what you see as pressure and stress might simply be your family's desire for you to make the most of what college has to offer. "Expressing your appreciation to your family for their support of your college career and sacrifices made on your behalf creates a sense of pride and respect for the family. Try to interpret and use these positive pressures as motivation to simply do your best," advises Thomas Worthy. "After all, your educational attainment will be one of the greatest honors you can bestow upon your family."

Making this shift, of course, is easier said than done. Fortunately, there are some specific tools and approaches you can use to make sure that you acknowledge your family's expectations without feeling restricted (or downright stressed-out) by them.

First and foremost, it's important to put out in the open—in your own mind, in conversations with your parents, and even with other family members—the expectations you feel coming from your family. Are there expectations about:

- What you should major in?
- How high you should keep your grades?
- What activities you'll be involved in?
- What you'll do after you graduate?

If so, acknowledge them. Admitting that, for example, your parents want you to major in business might do wonders for your stress levels, as stating something so plainly and so simply can sometimes calm down all the complicating factors you feel around the issue. Additionally, simply acknowledge or even ask for confirmation about what your family expects of you while talking in person, on the phone, or even over e-mail. If your parents expect you to come home every weekend or for every holiday weekend or break, state that you understand they want this to happen, or ask if they are indeed expecting this to be the case.

Understand Their Motivations

When acknowledging your family's expectations, it's important that you work to understand the motivations behind those expectations. Your family's desire that you major in business, for example, is likely motivated by their desire for you to have a good chance at solid, well-paying employment after graduation. And their desire to have you come home frequently and for long periods of time is possibly motivated by their worries that you'll separate from the family too much or, more simply, by the fact that they just really miss you. Understanding the reasons behind their expectations can help you better understand how to deal with them in ways that reduce the stress these same expectations might be introducing into your college experience.

Explaining Your Position

Once things become clearer, you can start to acknowledge what your family wants while also conveying your own preferences and desires. Okay, so your family wants you to major in a particular field—but you have a desire to major in something else. Try acknowledging what your family wants while also explaining how what you want meets a similar goal. Business may be their preference, for example, but majoring in a STEM field also provides job security, as there is a growing need for teachers. And your decision not to come home this weekend, for example, is being made not because you don't want to see them but because you want to be able to finish up a major research project so that, when you come home in a few weeks, you can really be mentally present during the visit.

Remember, You're Usually on the Same Team

Most families want what's best for their students. But sometimes, your family's own idea of what's best might be different than what you think is best. If everyone is working toward a similar goal and communicating well, a lot of stress can be avoided during an already stressful time. You can be aware of your family's expectations (and hopes and dreams for you) without feeling obligated to them.

When Parental Expectations Are Unreasonable

It's worth mentioning that some students do indeed feel—and, in fact, are—unreasonably restricted by their parents' expectations. If this is the case, the stress will be significant, and solutions to the situation and your stress will involve your breaking free from this kind of overmanagement and overinvolvement. You might want to talk with your academic adviser, a counselor, and financial aid staff members about what your options are if your parents are putting unreasonable demands on what you should be doing at school.

It is not fair, for example, for your parents to feel that, because they pay your tuition bills, they get to choose what you are studying. Do they have a say in what obligations you do have to meet—say, a certain GPA or not getting into trouble in the residence halls? Perhaps. But paying for your tuition bills doesn't warrant complete ownership and control of your experience. If this is the case, check in with people on campus about what your options are and how you can best deal with the situation. You don't want to be so stressed-out trying to meet unreasonable demands that your college experience and performance suffer. If your family's expectations have morphed into outright demands, it might be time to find other ways of supporting yourself during your time in school.

Solution #2: Forge Your Own Path

In an ideal situation, your parents would support you and provide nothing but positive reinforcement and guidance during your time in school. This, of course, rarely—if ever—happens.

College, however, is a major turning point in your life. You are transitioning to being an independent young adult who is making choices about what's best for your particular situation and for you as a person. At some point, you really do know what's best for you.

Your family's expectations can help inform that kind of self-awareness and self-knowledge, but they cannot create it for you. You know what makes your heart leap. You know what kinds of things get you academically and intellectually engaged and excited. You know what kinds of social activities and involvement leave you feeling refreshed, recharged, and re-energized. In essence, you know *you*. And part of what you're learning in college involves learning more about who you are and what makes you feel the happiest and most fulfilled.

While it's important to acknowledge and consider your family's expectations of you, it's incredibly important to choose your own path. It might feel uncomfortable and even scary to go against the grain of what your family is advising. And while following their suggestions might alleviate some stress over the short-term, it most certainly will exacerbate it over the long-term.

Because you know you best, you most likely also know what you really want your college experience to be like. And if you don't know, then the only way you are going to find out is to explore on your own—not listen to others, whether they're your family members or not.

One of the best ways to reduce your long-term stress while in college is to stay true to yourself. Major in what you want to major in. Be involved in what you want to be involved in. Learn more about the things you're curious about. Essentially, you need to create your own college experience, not live the one others expect for you.

Once you find yourself on this kind of path, your stress—the kind that lives deep, deep down in your belly—will likely reduce significantly. Trying to live your life for someone else is practically guaranteed to add enormous amounts of stress to your life. Take ownership of your own experience and your own choices. Learning to follow your heart and pursue your dreams may be scary and emotional at times, and it may even be stressful here and there. But it's also one of the most important life skills you can learn and, over the long-term, is also one of the best ways to avoid stress in your life. Once you start to chart your own course, you can reduce your stress, disconnect from past patterns that created stress, and start to establish your own patterns of living a healthy, positive, just-right-for-you life.

Solution #3: Remember How Staying in School Supports Your Family

On the surface, living your own purposeful, intentional life might seem selfish. It might seem that you are making choices based only on your own wishes and desires, thereby throwing your family's needs to the wayside.

This is both true and untrue. By following the passions of your own heart and mind instead of what your family thinks is best, are you being selfish? In the true sense of the word, yes. But this isn't necessarily a bad thing. Pursuing your own happiness is, in many ways, an obligation to yourself instead of an act of greed or inconsiderateness.

In college, you might feel like you have to choose between going to school and supporting your family. Your family may support your decision to advance your education, or they may judge you harshly. Either way, if you want to earn a college degree, it's worth it to try to make your best effort at doing so. Things may be difficult for you and your family during your time in school, but the benefits are likely to outweigh the drawbacks over the long-term. Graduating from college, after all, increases your earning power and your employability. You might be better able to support your family— or even your family's business—with the skills and training you learn as you work toward a degree. And just like many other long-term investments, a college degree requires short-term sacrifice:

- You may be absent from your family.
- You may not be able to contribute to your family financially or through your labor.
- The cost of your tuition and other school-related expenses might be a heavy burden.

You are also, however, an important member of your family, and you are supporting yourself and your own education by pursuing a degree. And when one member of the family benefits, everyone benefits. So while it can be difficult—and obviously very stressful—to pursue your college dream in the face of family hardship, keep your aim on the horizon. The long-term benefits are many, and the better and more focused you are in school, the more skilled and better equipped you'll be to help your family once you graduate.

Solution #4: Transform Family from Stressors to Motivators

Sometimes, no matter what you do, your family is just a stressful, stress-inducing mess.

If you can't change your situation, change how you react to it. If your family's pattern—in the past, currently, and most likely for the future— is to bring stress to your situation, regardless of the choices you make, what do you do now?

Perhaps the best approach you can take is to transform your family from a stressor to a motivator. Instead of feeling stressed-out when your mom tells you why you shouldn't be taking the classes you are, use your frustration as motivation to rock your classes and get amazing grades. Learn everything you can this semester so you can go home over the holiday break or summer, knowing that you not only made the right choices in the classes you took but that you also squeezed every last drop of knowledge out of your professors and course material that you possibly could.

✪ Straight from a Student: An Unsupportive Family

Stacy Serrano, a senior at San Diego State University, found herself dealing with family stress. For a variety of reasons, her family not only didn't provide much support during her time in school but also actively contributed stress and negativity along the way. At one point in time, Serrano remembers, "my parents and I were...not speaking at all and my younger brother had been told not to speak to me as well. I did not have much of a support system and going through the emotional distress of my parents' abandonment...led to the substantial downfall of my grades."

Despite Serrano's attempts to smooth things over with her family, things did not get better. "My relationship with my parents was not improving; they would not talk to me, except about business and bills,

206 College Stress Solutions

but every time we talked we would only argue. They always strived to pull me lower than I already was."

Clearly, this kind of family stress would have an impact on any student's experience in college—not to mention her chances at success. Ultimately, however, Serrano had to learn that if she couldn't adjust her family's attitudes and lack of support, she had to adjust the way she dealt with them. "All of these circumstances are out of my control, but what I have learned is that how I deal with these situations is under my control," she now recognizes. "My education is what will always help me become a better person and I will not allow myself to fail once more. Seeking support and asking for help is what has helped me tremendously at managing my stress levels." Instead of letting her family drag her down, she has learned to separate her own goals and dreams from the stresses her family introduces into her life. Serrano's most important realization, in fact, "has been to let go of all negativity...which includes cutting ties from family and so-called friends. Sometimes the hardest things to do are the most necessary to have an enriching life of your own."

If your family doesn't think you should be in school, use their disappointment (and the stress it's likely causing you) to propel yourself forward. Think of all the ways your life will be better with a college degree. Imagine how it will feel to toss your cap on graduation day. Picture how confident you will feel when walking into an interview for your dream job, knowing that you're there because of what you learned and experienced during your college days. Create an image in your mind of what your work environment will look like when you're older, with your diploma proudly displayed in a frame on the wall. Find joy in what the experience will be like when you reunite with your college classmates ten, twenty, thirty, or even fifty years from now.

If you can't change the stress your family is bringing into your life, try to learn new coping skills about how to handle it:

- Ask your friends what they do when their families makes them feel overwhelmed.
- Talk to your teammates about how they handle parental expectations that might border on ridiculous.
- Look online for articles and advice from both professionals and your peers about how to deal with family members who, intentionally or not, are somewhat sabotaging their students' college experiences.

You might be surprised to learn some of the coping mechanisms others use, and you might very well discover that some of these techniques can do wonders in your own life.

Additionally, if being in college presents you with opportunities that weren't or aren't available to other members of your family, use that as a great motivator instead of a stressor. Make the best of the chance you've been given to lead a different life and make different choices than other members of your family have. In some ways, you even owe it to your stress-inducing family to do your best with what you have, even if what you have is something they disagree with or don't approve of.

If you can't figure out how to prevent or deflect the family-oriented stress in your college life, turn it into an agent for change. Use it to motivate you, to remind you of what you want to be different in your life, to help you see a model of what you don't want to pass on to your own family members one day. Instead of feeling a lack of support from your family, use the stress they introduce into your life as the support itself. After all, if they can increase your angst and stress and energy levels, you can certainly do your best to transition that momentum into a motivator for positive choices and success.

Solution #5: Keep Your College Experience as Part of Your Family Life, Not Separate from It

Some days, you may simply wish for your family to disappear, and on other days, you might very well wish you could have them around more. Either way, you most likely can't completely ignore, get rid of, or change your family during your time in school.

Because your college experience is, in many ways, part of your family's experience, they're naturally involved to some degree. Your decision to go to school, and what you decide to do and study while there, all have a significant impact on each and every member of your family.

Plan Your Interactions Ahead of Time

These connections, however, will ideally work to support you during your time in school. One of the challenges you might face while in college is figuring out how much of your college life you'd like—or even need—to share with your family. Do your parents need to know everything you're doing on the weekends? Does that help you stay close, or is it causing more harm than good? Are they not approving of your choices and voicing that disapproval? Is your constant communication with them impeding your ability to connect with others and make friends?

On the flip side, calling or otherwise communicating with your parents as often as they'd like might feel like a serious pain. If you can agree on a regular date and time to talk, you might reduce your stress through a seemingly simple solution. Is talking to your parents one of the triggers for your stress? Perhaps. But if you know you only have to talk to them for twenty minutes or so on Sunday evenings, you can focus on other things during the rest of the week. You can plan in advance what you want to talk about so that you have some control over the topics that come up—and the stress they might otherwise introduce.

Additionally, while talking to your parents might add a little bit of stress once a week, *not* talking to them at regular intervals might add a great deal of stress when they call the campus administration, for example, to report you missing. Connecting to a family resource, even if it can be stressful at times, just might work to reduce your overall stress. You never know, after all, when your parents might have some insightful, helpful advice or when that twenty-minute phone call might be the highlight of your week.

Pick and Choose

It can be helpful to be choosy about which family members you interact with the most during your time in college. Your mother might stress you out, but your favorite aunt might be helpful at breaking down your stress into manageable levels. Your dad might be exceptionally skilled at making you feel stressed-out and guilty, but your big brother might also do wonders at helping put your dad's concerns in perspective and keeping you focused on and motivated toward your academic responsibilities.

Learning how your relationships with individual family members either add to or reduce your stress can help you strategize how best to interact with your family. Calling your aunt can be great for your self-esteem and your stress reduction, and, as an added bonus, she might calm your mother's fears about you during their own conversations. Reaching out more to your brother instead of your dad might improve everyone's relationships while helping you learn some great stress-reducing (not to mention dealing-with-Dad) tips along the way.

Ideally, you can utilize the family members who help you deal with and reduce your stress, while reducing your interactions with those who add stress. "Family" translates into a lot of different people and dynamics and relationships, all of which will contribute to your college experience in different ways. Don't be shy when it comes to being selective about who can best help you during your time in school—and who might be better for you to interact with a little less until you've achieved your dreams and graduated.

Solution #6: Keep Family Visits Positive and Enjoyable

Visits home present all kinds of funkiness during your time in school. In fact, you might be looking forward to your first visit home as a major break from starting college, only to discover that your visit is filled with conflict, miscommunication, and frustration.

Your First Visit Home

A student's first visit home is often surprising for both the student and his or her family. Everyone expects things to be the same when, in reality, nearly everything that affects your family's dynamics has completely changed in one way or another.

Even if you've only been away at school for a few weeks, you've undoubtedly experienced a degree of freedom that you didn't have when you were last at home. In college, you can come and go as you please, leave your room as messy (or clean) as you wish, and sleep when and for however long you want. You can also stay out as late as you want and not have to worry about letting people know your whereabouts.

Meanwhile, back at home, your parents have been adjusting to your absence. They might be used to a new schedule that doesn't involve having kids at home or that only focuses on a sibling left behind. Your siblings, too, have adapted to your absence, perhaps even moving into your room or suddenly being the focus of your parents' attention, whereas your transition to college had previously been stealing the spotlight.

Managing Expectations

Regardless of your family's particular dynamics, visits home can be both rejuvenating and challenging. And once again, these pros and cons all boil down to one thing: expectations.

You might be expecting to spend your visits home catching up on sleep, meeting up with friends you haven't seen, and otherwise doing things that don't involve your immediate family members. Your parents, however, might expect you to help around the house, spend time with the family, and treat them (and their car and the refrigerator) as more than just a bed and breakfast. How can you bridge a gap when both parties have such different, and seemingly conflicting, expectations of how visits home should go?

Even if you and your parents are taking opposing views about what should be happening during your visits home, you both are right. You are correct and justified in wanting a bit of your freedom and in wanting to spend at least some of your time doing your own thing. Your parents are also right. They are correct in assuming that, whether you are coming home for a long weekend or a holiday break, you will be more than just someone who pops in and out at all hours of the day (and night). You are, after all, a member of the family, too. And if you are going to be living with other family members, you need to respect and follow the rules that go with doing so.

Given all of this, the key to keeping home visits free of stress—for both you and your family—is to be very clear and talk upfront about what everyone expects:

- Is it okay for you to stay out all night and not tell your family where you are? This might work in college, but it might not work back home.
- Is it okay for you to take the car when you go out? How does that affect your parents' ability to, say, run errands or get to work the next morning?
- What kinds of events—from evening dinners to family reunions—does your family expect you to attend while you're at home? What are you expected to participate in and contribute to?
- How are your parents going to bend a little and adjust to the fact that you are becoming more independent? And how are you going to bend a little and adjust to the fact that, despite your developing independence, you still need to respect the rules of your family's household?

Talking these kinds of questions out will greatly assist you in avoiding complications. A visit home where you plan to sleep late, for example, can quickly turn stressful if your mom comes into your room and wakes you up so you can help with the yard work. And your parents' excitement about your coming home can quickly turn to frustration if you're never there to join them for dinner. It's important to talk about realistic expectations from both you and your family about what rules still need to be followed, how much you'll be expected to contribute, and what you'll need to make sure you can still cross things off of your college to-do list, like homework and study time, even though you're home for the weekend. Being home, after all, doesn't give you a pass on the college obligations that will be waiting for you when you return to campus.

Your Family's Visit to Your College

Conversely, it's important to have similar conversations for when your family members come to visit you, whether it be for Family Weekend or just for a quick visit. You don't want your family's visit to involve a lot of fighting, or to have them leave more concerned about you and your choices than they were when they first arrived.

To help make family visits to your school less stressful and more enjoyable for everyone, consider these tips:

1. Create some kind of schedule. Your parents are not likely to enjoy just hanging out in your residence hall, and you can't always guarantee that what they see while there will not be alarming.
2. Set up a campus tour or attend one that the admissions office has scheduled.
3. Have them meet some of your friends, maybe in the dining hall for lunch.
4. Try to take them off campus to see a museum, cultural event, or other fun activity, or attend a similar function on campus with them.

Things don't need to be scheduled down to the minute, as rigid schedules can often end up causing stress in and of themselves, but having a general idea of how you and your family will spend your time together can do wonders in making sure everyone has a nice time.

In essence, you'll want to show your family what your new life looks like while still acknowledging that you are—and always will be—part of the family you left behind. You want to give them an idea of whom you're hanging out with, what your routine looks like, and even where you go for things like classes and club meetings. Connecting your family to these kinds of details in your college life can, in essence, connect them to you and the person you are becoming. Their stress can be greatly reduced if they see how nice your friends are, how interesting your activities are, and what your schedule looks like on a daily basis. And when your parents or other family members know that you are doing well and thriving, they are much less likely to pass any family stress on to you during your time in school.

Family Stress: Conclusion and Highlights

While everyone experiences their family in a different way, having a family that sometimes (if not often) introduces stress into one's life is definitely a shared experience among college students. And even though your family dynamics can be both a cause and a solution to some of your stress, knowing how to proactively and reactively deal with these kinds of influences is key to making sure your family stress, while unavoidable, doesn't turn into an overwhelming obstacle.

- **Be honest with your family about your performance, potential, and possibilities.** Your family's expectations will weigh heavily on you during your time in school. Consequently, it's important to understand and acknowledge these expectations as well as their underlying motivations. If you can see where your family's expectations are coming from and respectfully address how your own capabilities and situations can still lead to your success, you can reduce the stress your family introduces.

- **Distinguish between acknowledging your family's expectations and feeling restricted by them.** Your family's expectations might be very similar to your own—but they can also be very, very different. Knowing what your family expects can be liberating because, once you understand that those expectations may or may not align with your own, you can acknowledge their presence while also feeling able to move in a different direction.

- **Follow your own dreams.** It can be tempting to agree to meet your family's expectations instead of following your own path, as doing so can avoid a lot of potential conflict and family discord. Over the long-term, however, you very likely might end up increasing your stress and overall unhappiness. Trying to live the life someone else has planned for you can be frustrating, stress inducing, and downright impossible. If you want to work toward having a life with less family-based stress, look inside yourself to find the things that will provide you with the most satisfaction and enrichment. Pride in your accomplishments and a feeling that you're in the right place and doing the right thing can be some of the best stress-busters imaginable.

- **Believe in yourself.** If you feel conflicted about having to choose between staying in school and supporting your family, take comfort in knowing that advancing yourself and your career prospects through a college degree is a worthwhile cause. There will be short- and even medium-term sacrifices, but sometimes the very best way to support your family over the long-term is to push through your challenges and doubts and stay in school.

- **Find the positive.** In situations where it just feels like, no matter what you do, your family is going to add stress to your college life, turn lemons into lemonade. Transform the stress your family is so good at creating into motivation. Let it remind you of why you're in school, what you hope to accomplish, and what life choices you'll make in the future.

- **Keep your college experience as part of your family life, not separate from it.** After all, your family is your family. No matter what you do or what happens in college, you're stuck with them—and vice versa. The challenge comes in finding a balance of how and when you'd like your college world and your family world to overlap. Figure out how much detail you want to share and how best to communicate with those family members who cause you stress. And learn to lean a little more on those family members who are supportive of you and your college journey. Because while your family as a whole may be stressful, there are likely a few family members who can greatly assist you—and reduce your stress levels—as you work toward your degree.

- **Manage expectations and schedules for family visits.** Expect that things will be different when you go home, whether it's your first visit home after being in school for a few weeks or it's your last visit home before you graduate. Be clear on what you expect from your family and what they expect from you. And if your family is coming to visit you, make sure you talk about expectations and are proactive about connecting them with your college life. It may just be that the best way to reduce the stress your family adds to your time in school is to show them that you really do have things under control, you really do know what you're doing, and you really are turning into the amazing person they always hoped you would become.

CHAPTER 8

Internal Stress

Amidst all the chaos of college—whether it be the academic, financial, personal, physical, social, emotional, or familial kind—sometimes the most stress-inducing, tumultuous causes of angst and anxiety come from one tiny place: within.

The pressure you put on yourself can be one of the most challenging factors in your college life. You may have expectations of what you can do, who you can be, and what kind of performance you will have. And if you don't meet those expectations or don't perform how you had hoped, you are your own worst—and harshest—critic.

Learning to balance your hopes and dreams with what you're reasonably able to achieve is a difficult skill, and one that often takes a lifetime to master. After all, you likely didn't head to college hoping to do poorly in your classes, struggle socially, and get deeply into debt. So if unexpected challenges present themselves, it can be difficult not to blame yourself.

Internal Stress: Identifying the Sources

You can most likely identify certain approaches, attitudes, beliefs, and patterns you have that contribute to your internal stress. After all, even the most positive people have bad days and feel frustrated with themselves from time to time.

Just like the other types of your college stress, the best way to find solutions to internal stress is to first identify the sources. While you are clearly the main source of your own internal stress, different dynamics are at play, and your internal stress may be stemming from various diverse triggers. Identifying them, as well as how they influence you and your internal stress levels, can be helpful in preventing them from causing harm down the road.

Internal Stress: The Five Questions

1. *What kinds of expectations do I have for myself for my time in college?* What do you hope to accomplish? What do you hope to feel proud of? What kinds of things do you want to do and experience? Do you truly believe you can achieve these goals, or does thinking about them stress you out? If so, how? How can you tell the difference between feeling internally stressed-out or just feeling nervous?

2. *Do I have a habit of stressing myself out?* If so, how does it begin? How do things get worse? How do things progress? What makes you keep adding to your own stress levels until you get to a high level of stress? Do you notice when you are starting to get stressed-out? Or do you only pay attention once you've reached a high level of internal stress? What thoughts or actions indicate that you're stressing yourself out? How do you know when you are becoming the source of your own stress? Are there any triggers that make you stress yourself out more?

3. *What am I most worried about during my time in school?* Academics, a social life, or just making it on your own? What kinds of things do you worry about most often during the

day? What kinds of things are you scared of doing? When talking (and listening) to yourself, do you speak kindly and encouragingly? Or do you harshly criticize yourself and speak negatively?

4. *Are there external triggers that make me internally stress out?* A certain situation? Your own behavior? A specific action- or performance-based stressor, like failing a test? What kinds of things do you worry about before they happen? What kinds of things do you worry about after they happen?

5. *How do I know if I'm stressing out about something instead of just working through it?* What kinds of thoughts and fears indicate you're internally stressed? What does your inner dialogue sound like when you're stressing yourself out? What does your inner dialogue sound like when you're just critically examining something? If someone else could hear how you talk to yourself, how would they know when you're stressed-out? What kinds of factors would they look for? What kinds of factors should you look for?

Finding Solutions

While your internal voice has much to do with your life choices, understanding how you might be undermining your own success is important if you hope to change your behaviors. Ideally, too, once you have reduced or even eliminated your internal stress, you'll be better able to enjoy the other aspects of your college experience.

Solution #1: Remember—You're Still YOU

While the requirements your professors have for their classes and the need to declare a major can cause stress, your own internal stress when it comes to academics can be just as heavy. You may expect yourself to meet a certain GPA, always perform well on tests, and impress your professors on every exam. If you were a high achiever in high school, you might be used to being an academic superstar. In college, however, you might suddenly be among your intellectual peers, meaning that your performance is now considered ordinary.

That kind of adjustment can be extremely challenging and, consequently, can cause quite a bit of internal turmoil. Travis Greene, Dean of Students at Grinnell College in Iowa, sees students struggle with this issue quite a bit. He notes that "one's perception of self or abilities can change dramatically when transitioning to college. In high school, many students were 'big fishes in a relatively small pond.'" A college environment, however, requires you to reassess your identity and self-perception, given this changed and changing context. In fact, Greene suggests, it's important that "students reframe how they view themselves—rather than feeling like they became small fishes in a big pond, we need to remind students they are the same big fish but help them understand that the pond has, indeed, become larger." So instead of focusing on how you might no longer feel academically or intellectually exceptional, realize that it's not you that has changed: it's your context.

Solution #2: Maintain Perspective

If you're extremely harsh on yourself about your academic performance, it might be time to take a deep breath and step back. While doing so is easier said than done, it's still helpful to keep some perspective. So what if others do better on an exam? Really…so what? If you still learned the material, performed well, and met other requirements (like a high enough grade to pass the class, stay in good academic standing, and keep your financial aid), then you did just fine. Wanting to be high achieving when it comes to your academics can be a great goal. But if you fall short of that goal, focus more on doing better next time than on turning the experience into a stressful one.

The consequences of your academic performance will, of course, vary depending on your individual situation. You may have certain scholarship requirements to meet, or your parents might have certain expectations for your performance. Your job as a college student, however, is to set academic goals based on what you want to learn and experience. If you find yourself having to function at a high level of internal stress all the time, you might not be having the college experience you had hoped.

Sometimes, the best thing to do is to take a deep breath and a step back. If your friend were in this exact same situation, what would you tell her? What would you advise? How would you encourage her to not be so harsh on herself? What tips would you give for how she could be kinder to herself and not stress herself out so much? Treat yourself like your own best friend and listen to what you'd share with someone else. It just might be the case that you are your own worst enemy, and, as such, you need to be more patient with yourself.

Solution #3: Adjust Your Expectations

Adjusting your expectations doesn't always have to mean lowering them. You just might end up achieving more, and reducing your stress, by changing what you expect out of yourself.

Your internal stress is both caused and affected by the expectations—especially the academic expectations—that you set for yourself. If you find that these expectations are not having a positive effect on your performance and are causing significant internal stress, then the problem is the expectations, not you. The only thing you are doing wrong is setting yourself up for stress that you, in essence, have complete control over.

✪ Straight from a Student: Defining Your Own Internal Happiness

While you might be your own worst enemy when it comes to causing internal stress, you just might also be your own best ally. Junior Vancea, a senior at the University of San Francisco, has learned to focus on what he personally needs to feel happy and fulfilled. Using his favorite quotation—"I make my own luck"—as motivation, Vancea knows that his sense of internal accomplishment comes from his "need to be more than just normal." Consequently, he motivates himself to reach out and connect with everyone from professors to future employers to friends, and to "not be afraid to be judged and criticized." While this may be challenging, Vancea notes that, "I need to do all these things in order to be internally happy. I am the type of individual that does not see any failure as a mistake, I see it as an opportunity for things I need to learn and do better. Therefore, I always seek help through the people and situations I encounter on a daily basis." By seeking out the interactions and experiences he finds to be internally rewarding, Vancea essentially transforms what could be internal stressors into internal motivators.

Remember, too, that your academic expectations and performance are your own. Forget everyone else, whether they're friends or family or classmates or study group partners. What performance do *you* want to have? What do *you* want to learn? What will allow *you* to meet your goals in a stress-free way that leaves you energized and excited on graduation day, not burned-out? When you let go of comparing yourself to others, you can let go of the internal stress that comes with such comparisons.

You are your own best ally and supporter. Don't sabotage your strengths and abilities by smothering them with self-imposed stress that could be avoided with a little adjustment of your expectations.

How to Tell if Your Internal Expectations Are Too High

You may very well feel a tension, however, between what you want to achieve and what you are able to achieve. Graduating *summa cum laude*, for example, is something you've always wanted to do. So what's wrong with having that expectation? Even if it causes you stress, it's still an important and lofty goal, right? Yes and no.

Recognizing the difference between high internal expectations and those that are out of reach can be challenging. Goals should be hard to accomplish, after all; there should be some struggle involved in trying to achieve them. That's why they're goals, not tasks.

In essence, your internal expectations should function more like hopes and goals instead of stress-inducing requirements. If you feel like you really want something and are eager to achieve it, then it can be a healthy goal. If, however, you feel like you absolutely must do something and become stressed-out at the idea of not being able to do it, then that is likely not a healthy goal. Realistic, achievable dreams can make you grow and strive and learn; unrealistic, unhealthy dreams can make you struggle, stress out, and feel like a mess when all is said and done. If your expectations and goals are causing more harm than good, it's time to adjust them.

You can also try asking yourself some important questions when it comes to analyzing whether your internal expectations and goals are serving a positive or negative function in your life:

- Can you realistically meet these expectations?
- What is the value behind each expectation?
- Can each expectation be achieved/added/lived in another way or through another goal that isn't so internally stress inducing?

Is your goal, for example, to be the top student in your department? Or is to always try your hardest and know that you are giving your academic program your absolute best? The former will undoubtedly cause all kinds of internal angst, especially because so much of it is not in your control; the latter can actually be quite empowering and stress reducing. After all, if you don't do so hot on a midterm, you might panic because it puts your "top student" status in jeopardy; if you know you studied as much and as hard as you could, you can feel proud of how you did on an obviously difficult exam. This simple change in perspective can do wonders for your internal stress and how you react to similar situations.

Your internal expectations should be constantly changing and helping you reach new levels. Don't keep internal expectations set in stone and otherwise inflexible. Those aren't internal expectations; those are stress-inducing requirements that are not beneficial to you, your experience, and your stress levels. Growth, learning, and even wisdom take time to happen. Be patient and kind with yourself as you go through the process.

Solution #4: Recognize the Difference Between High School and College

Much of your high school experience was probably focused on aiming to get into college. What classes you took, what clubs you belonged to, what volunteer work you did—it all likely was primarily focused around your goal of getting in and going to a good school.

Now that you're in college, however, everything has changed. You might not know what you want to major in, what you want to do for a career, or—on an more practical level—what classes to take and what clubs to join. Internally, this can lead to all kinds of self-imposed stress: What are you supposed to be doing? What is everyone else doing?

Because college is completely different from high school, your internal stress and even internal motivators will go through a rather significant recalibration. Going to class might be the only similarity between high school and college, yet even what constitutes "class" is completely different as well.

Try not to compare your high school experiences and performances to your college experiences and performances. You got into your college based on your high school achievements, but, more importantly, you also got in because of your potential. The only way to truly fail in college is to not make a serious effort to do well in most—if not all—of the aspects of your college life.

That effort, of course, takes place over a long period of time. You don't adjust to being in college within a week or two; it takes awhile and, consequently, it takes patience. Kurt C. Holmes, Dean of Students at The College of Wooster in Ohio, often has to remind students that, "You don't become a college student for weeks or even months. It has to be earned with hard work." In fact, Holmes tells students at his campus that, "The difference between high school and college is often agency. You 'had to' in high school; you 'chose to' in college. When a student asks if they have to do the reading, I often respond you don't have to do anything, you chose to come to Wooster; if you want to stay, you had better choose to do the work."

In college, after all, there is no longer one single goal. You aren't aiming for that golden college acceptance letter. In college, you are learning the skills you need to live an examined, aware life. Making yourself stress out about the smaller details of that process is a sure-fire way to miss the forest for the trees. Sure, you might feel some internal stress here and there about what you want to have happening and what you want to be doing. But that kind of stress should be minor, conquerable, and short-term.

Be Patient

In college, things are different. And internally, your stress will be different, too. Allow yourself time to adjust to the rhythms, requirements, and ebb and flow of being in college. You've been in high school for four years, so successfully immersing yourself in a completely different environment isn't going to happen overnight. You'll need to be patient with yourself as you learn your school's particular systems and cultures. And you'll need to be patient with yourself as you make mistakes along the way. Mistakes mean you're trying, and ideally you can view your mistakes as chances to learn something new instead of errors to stress out about or condemn yourself for.

Solution #5: Be Positive with Yourself

When you need to, you can probably tune out your family's pressure, your academic expectations, your financial obligations, and your social concerns. The one voice you probably can't shut off? Your own.

Sometimes, people tend to be their own worst critics. While falling asleep at night, for example, you might reflect on things you think you did wrong, things you think you should have done instead, and things you didn't get done but really should have prioritized. You might wish you could do something over or try again. One of the things that makes college life so wonderful and terrifying at the same time is that a lot of your choices and their consequences are long lasting and permanent.

When your stress starts to build internally, it can be incredibly helpful to learn how to say no to yourself.

- No, you don't need to obsess over what you should have done differently this weekend. Instead, focus on not repeating poor choices or behaviors.
- No, you don't need to panic about the grade you earned on your midterm. Acknowledge what you did wrong—and right—and decide to make appropriate changes in the future.
- No, you don't need to lose sleep worrying about what your parents are going to say when you tell them that you want to change majors. Stressing about what might happen is a waste of energy and often only sabotages what is going to happen.

You are in college because you are smart, focused, and driven. You know how to live an independent life and how to push yourself through difficult times. Those same skills, however, can backfire when you have difficulty letting yourself rest, relax, and recover. Learning to say no to that critical voice inside is challenging—but you can do it. Internal stress can feel like a tempest brewing. Try to take proactive steps to calm the storm, since internal stress is also something you have a lot of control over.

Focus on what you're doing right:

- You're in college and making progress.
- You're learning to live your life independently.

- You're managing living on your own, handling your money, going to class, and living an engaged and exciting life.
- You're balancing constant requests for your time and other resources, often without any kind of serious break.

It's okay to fail. It's okay to make mistakes. It's okay to say no when you are asking yourself to do too much. It's okay to realize you are sometimes being ridiculous and might need to change a lot of things in your college life in order to make your experience there more positive, productive, and healthy.

When you hear your inner dialogue starting to focus on the mistakes you make along the way, shut it down. Don't let your inner voice talk to yourself in a way you wouldn't tolerate from someone else. Learning to say no to the root cause of internal stress can be one of the most empowering ways to reduce your overall stress levels. And with that internal calm comes the ability to truly engage with and enjoy all that your college experience has to offer.

Internal Stress: Conclusion and Highlights

While often invisible to others, internal stress can quickly and easily become one of your biggest challenges during your time in school. The internal battles you have with yourself about what you should be doing, what should be happening, how you should be performing, and what your college experience is supposed to be like can be brutal. Consequently, exercising patience with yourself and working toward relaxing your internal expectations can do wonders for reducing your internal stress.

- **Set realistic expectations for your academics.** Set your goals based on what you want to learn and experience. Trying to meet the requirements or expectations of others will simply add more internal stress and may set you up for failure. When you can take ownership of what you want your academic experience to look like, you can focus on having that experience instead of stressing out about expectations that aren't your own.

- **Check in with yourself periodically to see if your internal expectations—and the internal stress that might be accompanying them—are too high.** Reasonable goals should help you learn, achieve, strive, and feel proud. Unreasonable goals can cause you to worry, stress, and feel like a failure, regardless of the outcome.

- **Acknowledge and be patient with yourself as you begin to understand the difference between high school and college.** Realize that this understanding may take your entire college experience to fully form. Instead of comparing your college self to your high school self, release this kind of internal tension and focus more on what kind of person you want to become. Your internal growth should focus on who you are naturally becoming, not on who you wanted to be.

- **Learn to say no to yourself.** Although you may not consciously realize it, your inner dialogue just might be one of the biggest stressors of your college life. If you feel yourself asking too much, learn to say no. If you feel yourself starting to stress out, learn to recognize those signs and put them to rest. If there's a part of you that has a tendency to add internal stress to your life, let it know that it is not welcome as part of your college experience. Focus on all of the things you are doing, learning, and succeeding at instead of putting more stress and pressure on yourself for all the things you wish you could be doing differently. You got this!

Index

About the Author

Kelci Lynn Lucier, EdM, has worked as a freelance education writer since 2008. Prior to working as a writer, Ms. Lucier worked at or for colleges for nearly ten years. She has a master's degree in higher education administration from Harvard University and a bachelor's degree in English & comparative literary studies from Occidental College.

Currently, Ms. Lucier is the College Life Expert on About.com and a cofounder of The College Parent Handbook website. Previously, she wrote *The College Experience* blog for *U.S. News & World Report*. She has been interviewed for or featured in multiple media outlets, including CNN's *Headline News*, Katie Couric's show *Katie*, TeenVogue.com, *CosmoGIRL!*, Yahoo! News, WSJ on Campus/Unigo, StudentAdvisor (a Washington Post Company), Her Campus, *LA Weekly*, the *Chicago Tribune*, the *Detroit Free Press*, the *Omaha World-Herald*, CollegeWeekLive, and the Association of College Unions International's *Bulletin*. She has also been featured as a guest on the *Growing Up with Dr. Jerry Brodlie* radio show and WCBS 880's *Opening Bell* in New York City. Additionally, she is a member of the Education Writers Association.